MORO
The Cookbook

MORO
The Cookbook

Sam and Sam Clark

Ebury Press

LONDON

First published in hardback in 2001
This paperback edition first published in 2003

1 2 3 4 5 6 7 8 9 10

First published in the United Kingdom in 2001 by Ebury Press
Random House, 20 Vauxhall Bridge Road, London SW1V 2SA

Random House Australia (Pty) Limited
20 Alfred Street, Milsons Point, Sydney,
New South Wales 2061, Australia

Random House New Zealand Limited
18 Poland Road, Glenfield, Auckland 10, New Zealand

Random House South Africa (Pty) Limited
Endulini, 5a Jubilee Road, Parktown 2193, South Africa

Random House UK Limited Reg. No. 954009

www.randomhouse.co.uk

A CIP catalogue record for this book is available from the British Library.

ISBN 0 09 187483 (hardback)
ISBN 0 09 188084X (paperback)

Art director and design: Caz Hildebrand
Editor: Susan Fleming
Photography: Pia Tryde
Picture research: Lily Richards

Papers used by Ebury Press are natural, recyclable products made from wood grown in sustainable forests.

Printed and bound in Italy by Graphicom SRL

CONTENTS

INTRODUCTION

Moro was born out of a desire to cook within the wonderful tradition of the Mediterranean, but with a need to explore new and exciting flavours. A fascination with Islam and a love of Spain and its people drew us to these less familiar areas of the Mediterranean. Linked in history by the Moors' 700-year occupation of Spain (from the eighth to the fifteenth centuries), the two spheres of cooking are connected by what we call the saffron-cinnamon link (Spain and the Muslim Mediterranean). We took the name Moro from the Spanish word for Moor, 'el Moro', which in itself is derived from the ancient Greek 'Mauros' meaning eastern.

So, before Moro opened in spring 1997, and newly married, we set out in a camper-van to drive through Spain and Morocco to the Sahara. The idea was to learn about as many flavours and techniques as possible and to try to discover details that really make food taste of where it comes from and not seem cooked by an Anglo-Saxon. This, combined with our experience at the River Cafe (simply cooked food and the importance of good ingredients), and our belief that vegetables should play as important a role as meat and fish, helped us produce plates that are unique to us. On our menus as within this book, the robust styles of Spanish cooking and the lighter, more exotic dishes of the Muslim Mediterranean hopefully make for a balanced and varied book.

The Moro cookbook is a distillation of our favourite recipes, a wonderful playground of tastes, conjuring up images of hairy-chested matadors and of hedonistic sultans. We hope, like us, you will be excited by these flavours and enticed by the romance and tradition inherent in each dish. We also want to impart something of the 'language of spice', how a teaspoon of ginger or five allspice berries can speak of different continents. Learn about spices and you can choose the accent to put on a simple dish.

In an attempt to give authenticity and depth to our food, we have ended up being surrounded by living things in the kitchen – we feed the culture for sourdough bread, we make live yoghurt daily, our wood oven and charcoal grill are fed continually, and a new member of the family – vinegar junior – is coming along nicely. In a short space of time our chefs build up relationships with these characters. At the risk of sounding like a 1970s health book, we would love to entice you into baking your own bread and making yoghurt.

It is important that you find it simple to put together Moro plates, which should be balanced, complementary and culturally true. We have been lucky enough to explore and to experiment, and have come up with a rich repertoire of dishes that are a little out of the ordinary. We hope you enjoy this book on many levels and take something from it that will last.

Sam and Sam Clark

BREAD

Three months before Moro opened, we turned our kitchen at home into a winter wonderland of flour as we set about trying to make sourdough bread. Inspired by San Francisco sourdough and the wonderful, large, rustic loaves from Puglia in southern Italy, we embarked on making a starter culture (natural leaven or yeast) from grapes. We nurtured this culture like a baby, feeding it three times a day until it was strong enough to breathe life into our dough. We watched it slowly transform what seemed like an unruly mass of flour and water into, in our opinion, no ordinary loaf of bread, but something rather special. However, our first loaves were not always successful, somewhat dense due to our impatience and lack of experience, but the more we understood and respected our dough, the better it became. Since then Moro bread is reputed to be some of the finest bread around, and although this sounds as though we are blowing our own trumpet, we are simply very proud of it.

WHAT MAKES GOOD SOURDOUGH?

Moro bread is everything a good sourdough should be – moist, chewy and slightly sour, with a proper crust. It has a much longer life than commercial bread and makes fantastic toast. However, it is more than just a normal sourdough and that is what makes it special, although it never ceases to amaze us how something so extraordinary can be produced from flour and water alone.

The choice of flour is crucial to the texture of good bread. At Moro we use Shipton Mill unbleached strong white bread flour that has a high gluten

content. There is no denying our wood oven also has its advantages. Not only does it give off a fantastic latent heat, but the loaves are baked directly on the stone floor and flavoured ever so subtly by the reassuring smells of wood ash. So what is the point of us going on about bread if you need a wood oven? Because we have devised a recipe that encapsulates the qualities of Moro bread that you can bake successfully and simply at home, and because we want to encourage as many people as possible to have a go. Do not underestimate the sense of satisfaction and achievement gained when you produce a loaf you are proud of.

THE CHEMISTRY OF BREAD

A little bit of science helped us understand how the miracle occurs when one mixes flour, water and yeast together. When kneading begins, the gluten in the flour is strengthened, producing sugars on which the yeast feeds. As a by-product of this process, carbon dioxide (among other things) is released and trapped in between the strands of gluten and causes the bread to rise.

When making bread at home it is not necessary to get bogged down with the meticulous details of temperature gauges, pH levels and digital measurements required for commercial bakeries. It is more important to get to know the character of your bread. We do not fuss over our bread – of course we respect it, but its beauty lies in its simplicity and in the accessible approach to how we make it. The result is that no batch, nor indeed loaf, of bread is the same, which we prefer as it gives it a unique quality.

Sourdough starter

Flour and water need yeast to turn them into bread. A sourdough starter or culture is an ancient form of yeast introduced more than 6,000 years ago, long before the arrival of brewer's yeast in the 1850s. However, what makes sourdough different from (and in our opinion superior to) brewer's yeast is that it is a natural, wild yeast. More specifically, sourdough is a combination of wild yeasts that both are airborne and exist in the flour, and acid-producing bacteria, which give it the slightly sour taste. The result is a more natural, slower process, and bread with a lot more character.

The sourdough culture we use at Moro is still the same one that we started before the restaurant opened, but this is a baby compared to some cultures. Puglia has sourdough cultures around 100 years old, handed down through the generations. A starter will stay alive for as long as you want it to, that is, as long as you keep feeding it, regardless of whether you make bread or not. A starter that is kept at room temperature must be fed every day, but to minimise the time you need to spend looking after it, we recommend keeping it in the fridge. This slows down the activity of the yeast so you need to feed it only once every week or two weeks (once if you make bread on a weekly basis or every two weeks if you do not). Between making bread, the starter will need a day of feeding to recover its strength.

TO MAKE THE SOURDOUGH STARTER
1 bunch organic red grapes
500g unbleached strong white bread flour (preferably organic)
1 litre water

To make our starter, we use grapes as they are a rich source of those wild yeasts and bacteria. Wash the grapes and wrap them in a muslin or fine cloth. Loosely secure the open end with string or an elastic band and lightly crush the grapes inside with a rolling pin. Mix the flour and water together in a plastic bucket, large ceramic or stainless-steel bowl (preferably with a lid), and squeeze some of the juice from the grapes into the mixture before submerging the muslin bag totally. Put the lid on or cover with a plate. Leave for ten days to two weeks at room temperature (about 20°C/68°F) until the grapes begin to ferment and the cloth inflates slightly with the gases that are given off. Raise the muslin bag just out of the mixture and squeeze any remaining juice back into the white mass, then discard the grapes and the bag. Give the starter a good stir. It should have a slightly pink tinge to it and a sour, grapey smell that can be a little unpleasant.

TO FEED THE STARTER (TWICE A DAY FOR 2 WEEKS)
100g unbleached strong white bread flour (preferably organic)
150ml water

First pour away approximately one-third (400ml) of the initial starter mixture and stir in the 'feeding' flour and water. Now start a system where-by you feed your starter twice a day, preferably at regular intervals, for two weeks.

Discard 200ml of the basic mixture before you feed the starter with the 100g flour and 150ml water. Although this may seem wasteful, you will otherwise end up with a huge amount of fermenting flour and water that is sure to take over your kitchen! After two weeks, taste a little of the starter on the tip of your tongue. If it has a slight fizz to it, it's alive! The mixture itself should have a healthy, very slightly active appearance, not bubbling necessarily, but looking alive. If the starter does not taste fizzy, keep feeding it until it does. It might just be a lower ambient temperature that is making the starter take a little longer. Now you are ready to make some bread.

LIVING WITH BREAD

Modern life does not lend itself very easily to baking bread, but we have endeavoured to make the process as simple as possible. Once you have taken the time and trouble to make the sourdough starter, you have a living thing on your hands, which does require a little looking after. We recommend you make enough bread to last you through the week (sourdough lends itself to this), which means you need only feed the starter once a week and leave it in the fridge for the rest of the time (see Sourdough Starter). Weekends are a good time to bake bread. You can make this bread by hand or in a mixer with a dough hook, and bake it in a bread tin. At Moro we use bread baskets, but this is not so practical at home.

A FEW TIPS BEFORE YOU MAKE BREAD

If you use a mixer with a dough hook, be careful not to over-mix the dough (5 minutes is sufficient). The gluten of an over-kneaded dough will have lost all its elasticity and this will result in bread of a poor texture and shape.

Bread needs warmth. It likes to be made in a modern centrally heated house, not a cold draughty pantry. Nowadays, most houses are warm enough, but do not leave the rising dough next to an open window. We sometimes cover our bread with a cloth if it is cool.

We use only fine sea salt, for salt crystals (unless they are dissolved in water) do not mix evenly.

Take the loaf out of its tin in the last 10-15 minutes of baking to form a good crust all over.

The slower the rise, the better texture and taste the bread has. For this reason we make our bread in two stages – first overnight and then the next day. This is best suited to sourdough especially.

Moro sourdough

What takes the time when making sourdough is the rising process. Excluding the baking time, the preparation should take about 20 minutes at each stage. This recipe will make two loaves. If, for example, you want to make bread at the weekend, this is how it would work.

STAGE 1: FRIDAY NIGHT, BEFORE YOU GO TO BED

> 450g unbleached strong white bread flour (preferably organic)
> 700ml cold water
> 250g Sourdough Starter (see page 12)

In a mixer, with a dough hook, or by hand in a large bowl, mix the flour, water and starter together until more or less smooth. Transfer to a larger bowl if the mixture comes above two-thirds, for it will rise a little bit. Cover and leave overnight.

Now feed the original sourdough starter

> 150g unbleached strong white bread flour (preferably organic)
> 250ml cold water

Add the flour and water to the original starter and mix with your hands until incorporated. It does not matter if there are a few lumps as these will disappear. Put back in the fridge.

STAGE 2: SATURDAY UP TO MIDDAY

> 450g unbleached strong white bread flour (preferably organic)
> 2-3 teaspoons fine sea salt (depending on how sour the dough is)
> olive oil or sunflower oil for oiling bread tins
> extra flour (bread or fine semolina) for dusting

You will need two 450g rectangular bread tins, roughly 22cm long by 11cm wide and 6.5cm high. Add the flour and salt to the existing bowl of dough that has been resting overnight and mix with your hand until smooth or turn the machine on to a low setting. When mixed in, beat by hand (with the tips of your fingers) for a good 5-10 minutes or continue in the machine for 5 minutes until more or less smooth and elastic. This dough does not need to be kneaded on a floured board, as it is too wet anyway. Rest for another 5-10 minutes to relax the dough. Beat again for a couple more minutes. Check for salt. A sourdough will need slightly more salt than bread made with commercial brewer's yeast because of its sour flavour. We always taste a little bit of the dough to make sure the balance is right.

Now prepare the bread tins. Oil them well, then dust the inside generously with flour (bread or semolina). Divide the dough and fill each tin just over half, but no more than two-thirds, full. Dust the top with more flour. Depending on the room temperature and activity of the starter, the dough will need 3-5 hours to prove until increased in size by a third at least, or the dough has risen just over the top of the tin. To see if it is ready, press your hand gently on top of the dough. It should feel light and airy.

STAGE 3: SATURDAY AFTERNOON

When the dough is roughly in its last hour of rising, preheat the oven to 230°C/450°F/Gas 8.

When the oven is up to temperature and you are satisfied the dough has risen sufficiently, place the tin on the middle shelf. Bake for a good 30 minutes (try not to give in to the temptation to look at it for the first 15 minutes as it can affect the rise). When the 30 minutes are up, remove the bread from the tins and bake for a further 10-15 minutes. If the bread has formed a good hard crust and has browned it is ready. To make extra sure, tap the bottom, which should feel hollow.

Transfer to a cooling rack and leave until completely cool. It is always tempting to cut the bread before it has totally cooled, but if you do, the steam will be released and change the texture. Bread with a perfect texture should have even holes and a glossy look to it. If your bread is split or cracked in any way, then it means it had not quite proved enough.

Bread with brewer's yeast

At Moro, we tend to make bread with brewer's or commercial yeast on Monday mornings for two reasons. As Sunday is our day of rest, we are unable to put on a batch the night before and our wood oven, which has cooled down completely, cannot get up to temperature in time.

Makes 2 loaves
> 700ml tepid water
> 1 kg unbleached strong white bread flour (preferably organic)
> 1 level teaspoon dried yeast, dissolved in 125ml tepid water
> 2 level teaspoons fine sea salt, to taste

You will need two 450g rectangular bread tins of 22cm long, 11cm wide and 6.5cm high. Yeast bread does not require two rises. Simply mix all the ingredients together, beat until smooth (like the sourdough) and transfer to the prepared bread tins (see page 16). This bread will also take less time to rise, about 3 hours. When you are satisfied it is ready, follow baking instructions exactly for the sourdough bread. Yeast bread does not last as long as sourdough, but it is still very good.

Flatbread

Although our sourdough is the bread we hand round to our customers, we often make flatbread to accompany certain dishes, such as mezze. Again our flatbread is baked in the wood oven, but it is easy to bake in a domestic oven, although it takes a fraction longer. Before we bake the flatbread we lightly oil the top and sprinkle it with either za'tar (see page 154) or other dry spices such as nigella (see page 40) or sesame seeds.

Makes 4 breads
> 200g unbleached strong white bread flour (preferably organic),
>   plus a little extra for dusting
> ½ teaspoon fine sea salt

⅓ level teaspoon dried yeast

170ml tepid water

1 tablespoon olive oil, plus a little extra for greasing

Place the flour and salt in a large mixing bowl. Dissolve the yeast in the water and then pour the oil into the water. Now pour the water into the flour a bit at a time while mixing. We like to do this by hand, squelching out the lumps as they appear. When all the water is added, transfer to a floured surface and knead well. If the dough is very sticky add a little more flour; if it is still crumbly add a little more water. Continue kneading for about 5 minutes until the dough is ever so slightly tacky, but soft, elastic and smooth. Set aside to rest for 45 minutes on the floured surface covered by a cloth.

Preheat the oven to 230°C/450°F/Gas 8.

Divide the dough into four, and roll into balls. On a generously floured surface, with a rolling pin gently roll each ball to approximately 3-5mm thick, making sure the shape is a rough circle about 15-20cm in diameter or oval about 15cm in length. Place on a flat, oiled baking tray and bake in the top of the oven for about 5-10 minutes. Each bread should partially bubble up and colour slightly yet not be totally crisp.

Moroccan bread

Rounds of this bread are served with some of our Moroccan recipes such as Lentil Soup with Cumin (see page 76) or mezze.

Makes 4 breads

- 300g unbleached strong white bread flour (preferably organic)
- 1 teaspoon fennel seeds
- a good pinch of salt
- ½ teaspoon dried yeast, dissolved in 1 tablespoon warm water
- ¾ teaspoon runny honey
- 225–250ml milk
- a little olive oil
- 1 egg yolk, mixed with 1 tablespoon milk, to glaze

Mix the flour, fennel seeds and salt in a large bowl. Add the dissolved yeast and the honey. Now pour the milk into the flour a bit at a time while mixing. We like to do this by hand, squelching out the lumps as they appear. When all the milk is added, transfer the dough to a floured surface and knead well. If it is still sticky add a little more flour; if it is still crumbly add a little more milk. Continue kneading for about 5 minutes until the dough is a little tacky, but soft, elastic and smooth. Set aside to rest for 1 hour on the floured surface covered by a cloth, until doubled in size.

Preheat the oven to 230°C/450°F/Gas 8.

Divide the dough into four, and roll into balls. On a generously floured surface with a rolling pin, gently roll each ball to approximately 1.5cm thick, making sure the shape is a rough circle about 12–15cm in diameter. Place on an oiled baking tray, and pinch your index around the centre of the bread twelve times, which looks nice and slightly restricts rising. Brush the top with the egg glaze, and bake for about 15–20 minutes or until the dough has risen slightly, is golden in colour and sounds hollow when tapped on the bottom.

TAPAS AND MEZZE

There is something about sharing little morsels of food with friends that brings an unselfconscious intimacy and sociability to the occasion. Tapas and mezze represent not only national styles of eating in Spain and the countries of the Muslim Mediterranean respectively, but an important part of the way of life.

TAPAS

Our first tapas experience was very special. We were taken to the best bars in Granada by our friend Lidia, where we sipped sherries or quenched our thirst with ice-cold 'cañas' (beers), and for every drink, there was always an imaginative array of tasty things to eat. This is what the Spanish call 'tapear'; for us, it was an unforgettable evening of warmth, conviviality, and fun. It was, in fact, our first taste of Spain and perhaps one of the reasons why we immediately fell in love with the country, its culture and people.

Tapas originated in the south at the beginning of the nineteenth century in the form of a slice of bread or sausage literally to cover, 'tapar', one's glass either to keep the insects away, or to stop drinkers getting too tipsy. Andalucía was and is the home of sherry, and the two went hand in hand. A glass of sherry and a tapa soon became customary, and it was not long before the tradition spread out from Andalucía to the whole of Spain.

Tapas come in many forms, from a simple plate of salted almonds to more elaborate, cooked dishes such as 'calamares en su tinta' (squid in black ink). There are also two sizes to choose from – 'tapa' or the larger 'ración' – and as well as staple dishes that appear on blackboards in most tapas bars, there are just as many regional specialities and variations.

In this chapter we have chosen mostly simple tapas to reflect this social tradition of a few nibbles with a drink as a prelude to a main meal, like the tapas we serve at the bar at Moro. However, if you want more choice, many of the starters in this book are originally tapas dishes, which can easily be adapted back by simply halving the quantities.

Almendras con pimentón
ROAST ALMONDS WITH PAPRIKA

This is a delicious accompaniment to a glass of chilled fino sherry. The taste of smoked Spanish paprika and lightly roasted almonds is surprisingly complex.

Serves 6

    250g whole blanched almonds (see page 56)
    1 teaspoon olive oil
    1 teaspoon smoked sweet Spanish paprika (see page 111)
    1½ teaspoons sea salt (preferably Maldon), ground to a powder as
       fine as icing sugar

Preheat the oven to 150°C/300°F/Gas 2.

Place the almonds on a baking tray and dry-roast in the top of the oven for about 25 minutes or until golden brown. Remove and stir in the olive oil, paprika and salt. Return to the oven for another couple of minutes. Remove and cool before eating.

Tortilla

At Moro, we always make a tortilla for the bar. For us it encapsulates much about Spanish food, and if done well is a miraculous thing. The secret of a good tortilla lies in the sweetness of the onions and the luxurious softness of the potatoes.

Serves 6-8

> 2 large Spanish onions
> 700g potatoes (Cyprus or any firm, waxy potato)
> 10 tablespoons olive oil
> 750ml sunflower oil for deep-frying
> 6 eggs, organic or free-range
> sea salt and black pepper

Cut the onions in half, peel and thinly slice. Peel the potatoes, cut in half lengthways, and then across in slices 5mm thick. Toss with ½ teaspoon salt and leave to stand in a colander.

Heat the olive oil in a large heavy saucepan and when hot but not smoking add the onions with a pinch of salt. Give them a good stir, reduce the heat to low, and cook very slowly for about 30-45 minutes until golden in colour and sweet in smell. Be sure to stir the onions every 5 minutes so they cook evenly and do not stick to the bottom of the pan. Remove from the heat, drain, and reserve the oil.

Meanwhile, cook the potatoes. A deep-fat fryer is perfect but for those without one, pour the sunflower oil into a similar-sized saucepan (never fill the pan more than half full) and set over a medium heat. The temperature is crucial as the potatoes should cook until tender without colouring, that is, simmer gently and not spit furiously. Drain in a colander. Strain the oil and keep it back for another occasion.

Break the eggs into a large mixing bowl and whisk briefly. Add the onions and potatoes and mix together. Taste for seasoning. The mixture may only need a little pepper.

Pour the reserved onion oil into a frying pan approximately 20cm across, and set over a high heat. When the oil begins to smoke pour the mixture in with one hand whilst shaking the pan with the other. Reduce the heat

to low and cook for 3–5 minutes or until the underside is golden brown. Then take a plate of a similar size and rest it over the pan. With both hands and two kitchen cloths carefully invert the tortilla on to the plate. The uncooked side will still be fairly runny so watch out! Turning the tortilla helps to give it its distinctive shape.

Turn the heat to high again, pour a little extra olive oil into the frying pan and slide the tortilla back into the pan runny side down and tuck in the edges. Cook for another 3 minutes. Both sides of the tortilla should now be golden brown in colour. If not, it requires a little more cooking. The tortilla will be cooked if the middle feels solid. If it still feels a little soft, continue to cook until firmer. Remove from the pan and slide on to a plate. Allow to cool for a few minutes before cutting into diamond shapes.

Aceitunas aliñadas
MARINATED OLIVES

We like to use a combination of olives for a variety of textures, colours and tastes. Firm green ones, 'petit lucques', for a slightly crunchy texture, black oily ones, 'douces' or 'thrombes', that are dried on the vine for intensity of flavour, small brown 'arbequina' and black 'niçoises' for a thinner skin, and plump, juicy purple ones, 'tailladées' or 'kalamata'. It is up to you what you like and what you can find.

Serves 4

350g mixed olives in brine (see Suppliers)
1 teaspoon coriander seeds
1 garlic clove, very thinly sliced
zest and juice of 1 orange
1 teaspoon fennel seeds
a few black peppercorns
1 large fresh red chilli, halved lengthways, seeded and finely chopped
½ small bunch fresh flat-leaf parsley leaves, roughly chopped
4 tablespoons olive oil

Drain the olives of their brine, rinse briefly, and place in a bowl with all the other ingredients. Stir well and leave to marinate for at least an hour.

Pimientos del piquillo
PIQUILLO PEPPERS

 The name 'piquillo' comes from the word 'pico' meaning 'little tail' as its shape suggests. Piquillo peppers are grown in the Navarra region of Spain. Although smaller than the bell pepper (only about 8cm in length), they are however much superior in flavour, texture and colour. The majority of piquillo peppers are harvested in October, roasted over beech wood, peeled (the best quality by hand) and then tinned in their own juice. They are sweet (and sometimes mildly spicy), bursting with flavour, and are perfect for stuffing, for sauces or simply for a tapa. You can now buy them in some delicatessens and super-markets, though they are expensive partly due to production costs. (See Spanish Suppliers)

Pimientos del piquillo aliñados
MARINATED PIQUILLO PEPPERS

At the restaurant we marinate piquillo peppers very simply with garlic, sherry vinegar and parsley. They are delicious on their own or a perfect complement to tortilla or a salted anchovy.

Serves 4

      225g piquillo peppers (see above)
      1 garlic clove, thinly sliced
      1 tablespoon sherry vinegar
      2 tablespoons olive oil
      a handful of roughly chopped fresh flat-leaf parsley
      sea salt and black pepper

Drain the peppers of their juices. You can either leave them whole, or tear them roughly into thirds. Toss them with the rest of the ingredients and leave for a good half-hour to let the flavours mingle.

Boquerones fritos
DEEP-FRIED ANCHOVIES

When we see the words 'boquerones fritos' on a tapas board we cannot resist ordering a plate of these sweet, succulent fish. Simply fried in flour and served with lemon, the Spanish occasionally prepare them in fan shapes. Fresh anchovies are available in this country and if we can get them in the restaurant, there is no reason why your fishmonger can't!

Serves 4

    1 kg fresh anchovies, heads on or off and gutted
    750ml sunflower oil, or a mixture of sunflower and olive oils
    100g plain flour (or fine semolina flour for crunch)
    1 lemon, quartered
    sea salt and black pepper

About 15 minutes before frying, lightly salt the anchovies. Heat the oil in a large saucepan until hot but not smoking (never fill the pan more than half full). Mix the flour in a large bowl and season generously. Toss the anchovies a few at a time in the flour and dust off any excess. Fry in batches; they should take no longer than 30 seconds, but test one to see. Drain on kitchen paper and serve immediately with the lemon.

Anchoas, boquerones, anchovies

Anchovies are enjoyed with great relish throughout Spain – fresh, salted and marinated. The name 'boquerón', meaning 'big mouth', alludes to the anchovy's protruding upper jaw, and is also used for the fresh and pickled fish whereas the salted ones are known as 'anchoas'. Some 90 per cent of Spain's anchovy production comes from the Bay of Biscay. The season starts from March or April, peaking during the summer. When each catch comes in, the individual fish are immediately graded by size and selected for salting, pickling or selling fresh accordingly. The Turks are also great lovers of anchovies, which they call 'hamsi'. (See Spanish Suppliers)

Boquerones en vinagre
MARINATED ANCHOVIES

'Boquerones en vinagre' are a staple tapa in bars throughout Spain, but the best to be found are around Cantabria and parts of Andalucía where the fish are caught. Boquerones are anchovies pickled in vinegar (usually white wine vinegar or sherry vinegar in the south). The quality can vary widely, but look for the plumpest, juiciest, whitest flesh. In the north of Spain, especially in the Basque country, tapas are often served as 'pinchos' or skewers, and we have often enjoyed many a pincho of an anchovy with a caperberry, and a pickled chilli. Punchy but addictive.

Serves 4

    8 boquerones fillets, drained of their oil (see Spanish Suppliers)
    8 whole flat-leaf parsley leaves
    8 green pickled chillies, cut in half across
    8 caperberries

Lay out each anchovy fillet, silvery side down. Place the parsley leaf at one end and roll up. Secure with a cocktail stick and spike a pickled chilli at one end and a caperberry at the other. For the real experience, eat in one mouthful. A pincho of a salted anchovy is also delicious, but instead of the pickled chilli use quarters of a piquillo pepper. Or substitute the cocktail stick with a piece of bread to make a 'mondatido', a tapa on a piece of bread.

Chorizo al jerez
CHORIZO WITH SHERRY

With chorizo you can normally choose between the mild, sweet variety – 'dulce' – and one that is slightly spicy – 'picante'.

Serves 4

    200g chorizo suitable for cooking (see page 112)
    olive oil
    75ml fino sherry

Cut the chorizo in half lengthways and then into little bite-sized pieces. Place a frying pan over a medium heat and add a few drops of olive oil. You don't need very much as the chorizo will release its own oil. When the pan begins to smoke, add the chorizo and fry, turning quickly when one side is coloured. This will take a matter of seconds. When both sides are crispy, add the sherry, watch out for the hissing, and leave for a few seconds to burn off the alcohol. Transfer to a dish and enjoy immediately. You can grill these chorizo just as easily, but omit the sherry.

Pan con tomate y jamón
BREAD WITH TOMATO AND CURED HAM

Catalan in origin, bread with tomato and jamón (cured ham) is a Spanish institution which we believe everyone must try. We were in Murcia, in a small bar near the centre of town. It was eleven o'clock in the morning and the bar was full of men drinking their usual cerveza or café con coñac or 'carajillo'. We ordered two 'pan con tomate y jamón', the house speciality: a fresh roll cut in half, generously rubbed with garlic and sweet tomato, drizzled with fruity olive oil and covered with thin slices of a good-quality jamón (see page 116). It was one of our most memorable breakfasts ever. There were tiny cubes of jamón fat in the roll, which made it even tastier. Good bread, toasted or fresh, is important. Try sourdough, ciabatta or a crusty roll, and choose the sweetest tomatoes when they are in season. We also like to grate the tomato, mix it with garlic and olive oil and spread it on the bread. Salted anchovies on tomato toast is also delicious.

Serranitos

We are very fortunate to be able to work with a few Spanish people at Moro. We always enjoy listening to them talk about their favourite things to eat, usually cooked by their mothers. Borja Flores Barroso from Jerez told us about a tapa he enjoys around 'feria' – or festival time – in May. It is called a 'serranito' because it comes from the sierra, or mountains. It is a simple, but delicious combination of flavours, rather like the Italian 'saltimbocca', and like saltimbocca it certainly 'jumps in the mouth'.

Serves 4

- 1 x pork fillet, about 400–500g, cut across into 8 slices and flattened with a knife
- 1 garlic clove, crushed to a paste with salt
- ½ teaspoon sweet smoked Spanish paprika (see page 111)
- 2 green bell peppers, or Spanish or Turkish 'goat's horn' peppers
- 10 tablespoons olive oil
- 8 slices ciabatta bread or baguette, cut on the diagonal, or 4 slices Moro Sourdough (see page 14)

thin slices of jamón serrano (cured ham), about 70g (see page 116)

sea salt and black pepper

To marinate the pork, rub the garlic, paprika and freshly ground black pepper all over and set aside for a good half-hour.

Meanwhile prepare the peppers. For the bell peppers, cut in half lengthways and gently pull out the core and seeds. Now cut each half into half again. If using the smaller Spanish or Turkish variety, leave whole. Set a frying pan over a medium heat and add half the olive oil. When the oil is hot, add the peppers and fry on both sides until soft. Season and set aside.

When you are ready to eat, lightly toast the ciabatta, baguette or sourdough. Add the remaining oil to the pan and set over a medium flame. When the oil begins to smoke add the pork and quickly fry on one side for about a minute and turn over. Fry for another minute until cooked through but still juicy. Turn off the heat and season the meat well. Immediately transfer the fillets on to the bread, followed by the pepper and then the jamón. Grind on a little black pepper and eat immediately.

Queso Manchego con membrillo
MANCHEGO WITH MEMBRILLO

Little preparation is involved in this tapa but the combination of Spain's most famous cheese and a paste made from quinces is worth mentioning. A hunk of good bread, a few slices of Manchego and slivers of sweet, fruity membrillo is a perfect combination, especially when accompanied by a glass of nutty, dry oloroso sherry.

Serves 4

400g Manchego (see Spanish Suppliers)

200g membrillo (see page 34 and Spanish Suppliers)

Traditionally Manchego is served in triangles. Each triangle should be the shape of an eighth of the entire cheese and each slice no more than 5mm thick. Keep the rind on. For the membrillo, slice in wedges 5cm long, 1cm wide and 5mm thick. Place the membrillo in the middle of each triangle of Manchego (see photograph on page 23).

Make your own membrillo

 The quince is an old-fashioned fruit that grows well in Britain. In the autumn, try making your own membrillo. Cut up approximately 2 kg quinces, place in a large saucepan and cover with cold water. Bring to the boil, then simmer until the fruit is soft and can be mashed. Strain off any excess water and put the quinces through a mouli or sieve, getting rid of any core or pips. Weigh the purée and measure out an equal quantity of sugar. Place both the sugar and purée in the same (but washed) saucepan and return to the hob over a low heat. It is necessary to stir the mixture almost constantly, otherwise it might catch and burn. Let it bubble slowly (trying not to burn your stirring arm) until it has turned deep maroon in colour. This can take a while. Taste and add some lemon juice if it is very sweet. Pour on to a tray or dish lined with grease-proof paper, to a depth of 2–3cm. Put in a warm, dry place to cool completely and set.

Jerez
SHERRY

Saying one does not like sherry is like saying one does not like wine after trying Blue Nun. Sherry comes in a world of different styles, from the light and dry to the dark and deliciously rich, and each style contains a whole spectrum of flavours.

Sherry starts its life as a simple wine that goes through what is called the 'solera system'. This was originally a Roman technique for blending wines from different years in the barrel to give consistency over the vintages so there was little fluctuation in quality due to bad weather and so forth. This technique is also what gives sherry character, for the wine itself (most usually made from the Palomino grape) is simple, not to say down-right boring.

In this time of easy-to-drink young wines, we have become huge fans of sherry. We know that for some 'sherry' is a dirty word, but we have been swept away by the complexity of its tastes and the romance of its production. This latter hinges on two things. One is the 'flor', or mother fungus, that lives on the fino and manzanilla wines and gives them much of their distinctive quality. The wines are alive and kept fresh until they are taken away from their mother and bottled. This is wonderful: a living organism that shapes as well as preserves this wine in the barrel! The other romantic aspect that we appreciate is the lineage acquired in every bottle of sherry. Because of the solera system, part of what you are tasting may be two years old, but part may be two hundred years old. You are tasting a wine from another age, another time, with depth and personality to match.

Great wines have the ability to affect one emotionally, but these wines are few and far between, and are often subject to extortionate prices or fluctuations in vintages. In our opinion, numerous sherries come under the 'great wine' banner, yet they are comparatively excellent value. Now is the time to forget the word 'sherry' and instead familiarise yourself with the 'bodegas' (sherry houses) and enjoy the noble styles of fino, manzanilla, manzanilla pasada, amontillado, palo cortado, oloroso and Pedro Ximénez. For a description of each style, a list of our favourite sherries and where to source them, see Sherry Suppliers.

MEZZE

Mezze are an integral part of life in much of the Muslim Mediterranean, and as with tapas, provide one of the most civilised and exciting ways to eat. At the restaurant we fit many mezze on to one plate. This is fine but the real joy of mezze is the array on the table and the sharing. We have put together some dishes from Morocco, Turkey, Egypt and Lebanon. Many are distinct to their region, yet there is still a crossover in tastes and textures that give a harmony within the selection.

At home, creating a mezze spread out of eight to ten dishes is not something you could do the whole time, but now and then it is a fun and memorable way to share food. Here are some tips we try to follow when making mezze:

- Think seasonally when it comes to the vegetables (see page 283).
- Invite friends or family to help with some of the preparation. Mezze should be social to prepare as well as to eat.
- Always bear mezze in mind when thinking of a picnic or barbecue.
- For authenticity and sensuality eat with your hands, scooping up the food with warm Flatbread (see page 18).

A good selection and balance of tastes, textures and colour might be as follows:

Grilled chicken wings with tahini
Falafel
Tabbouleh
Beetroot with yoghurt
Spiced labneh
Wilted herb salad
Fava bean purée
Carrot and cumin salad with coriander
Crudités: carrots, celery and radishes
Olives, pickled chillies, pickled turnips
Flatbread

Quails' eggs with cumin

In Morocco, we often ate hard-boiled eggs with cumin sold on street corners or offered around as we sipped mint tea in a café. This classic combination reminds us of a tapa we ate in Granada: fried quails' eggs also sprinkled with cumin. The recipe below originates from these two occasions.

Serves 4

      1 dozen quails' eggs

      1 teaspoon sea salt (preferably Maldon), finely ground

      2 teaspoons cumin seeds, lightly toasted (see page 41)

Boil the quails' eggs for 4 minutes. Remove and cool. Mix the sea salt and cumin together in a mortar and pestle and grind. As you peel each egg, dip into the salt and cumin mixture for every mouthful.

Grilled chicken wings with tahini

This is a classic Lebanese dish, perfect for the barbecue.

Serves 4
> 12 chicken wings, tips removed
> Tahini Sauce (see page 255)
> 1 small bunch fresh flat-leaf parsley, leaves picked from the stalks
> 1 lemon, quartered
> sea salt and black pepper

MARINADE
> 3 garlic cloves, crushed to a paste with salt
> 1 teaspoon paprika
> 1 teaspoon freshly ground cumin
> juice of 1 lemon
> 2 tablespoons tahini paste
> 1 tablespoon olive oil

In a large bowl, mix together the marinade ingredients. Add the chicken wings, making sure they are well coated, and leave to marinate for at least an hour.

A barbecue is an ideal way to cook the wings, or alternatively use a hot grill, griddle or oven (the latter at 220°C/425°F/Gas 7). Cook for about 15 minutes, turning occasionally until the skin is golden brown and slightly charred and the meat cooked through. Check for seasoning. Serve with tahini sauce, parsley leaves and wedges of lemon.

Beetroot with yoghurt

This is a classic dish that adds vibrant colour to any mezze spread. When beetroot are in season you may come across the golden and stripy varieties. While not entirely traditional, a combination of these can make this dish even more startling. Nigella (or black onion seed) is an aromatic, charcoal-black seed similar to black sesame in shape. It is sprinkled on yoghurt and flatbreads, especially in Turkey.

Serves 4

    500g beetroot
    a squeeze of lemon
    1 tablespoon olive oil
    1 small bunch fresh flat-leaf parsley leaves, roughly chopped
    sea salt and black pepper

TO SERVE
    1 garlic clove, crushed to a paste with salt
    200g home-made or Greek yoghurt, thinned with 2 tablespoons milk
    olive oil
    ½ teaspoon nigella seeds (see Turkish Suppliers or some Indian
        shops)

Wash the beetroot carefully without piercing the skin otherwise they will bleed. Place in a saucepan of cold salted water and bring to the boil. Depending on the size of the beetroot, it will take anywhere from half an hour to an hour. They will be ready when you can slip a sharp knife easily into the centre, rather like testing to see if a potato is cooked. Drain and rub away the skin with your fingers under a running cold tap. If the beetroot is cooked the skin should come away very easily. Cut into 1cm rounds, arrange on a plate, and dress with the lemon juice, olive oil, parsley, salt and pepper.

Mix the garlic with the yoghurt and check for seasoning. Pour over the beetroot, drizzle with a little olive oil and sprinkle on the nigella seeds. We also serve this dish warm, as it is delicious with grilled fish or chicken. The beetroot bleeds into the yoghurt, turning the sauce bright purple.

Carrot and cumin salad
with coriander

For us the secrets of this Moroccan salad are good-quality carrots, organic if possible, and lightly pan-roasting the cumin.

Serves 4

 450g carrots
 2/3 teaspoon cumin seeds
 1 garlic clove
 juice of 3/4 lemon
 1/3 teaspoon caster sugar
 1 tablespoon olive oil
 1 small bunch fresh coriander leaves, roughly chopped
 sea salt

Peel the carrots and boil whole in salted water until they are tender. Drain the carrots, spreading them out to cool and dry before slicing them quite thinly.

To roast the cumin seeds, place in a small saucepan and stir over a medium heat until you notice the colour beginning to change (about 2 minutes). Pound the cumin in a mortar and pestle, then add the garlic and 1/2 teaspoon salt and pound some more. Mix the lemon juice, sugar and olive oil into the garlic mixture. Now toss the carrots in the cumin dressing with the chopped coriander. Serve at room temperature.

Aubergines with garlic, mint and chilli

The secret of this recipe is to fry the aubergines until deep brown as this gives them a wonderful caramelised, nutty flavour, which improves with age. Serve with warm Flatbread (see page 18) and yoghurt seasoned with salt and pepper.

Serves 4

- 3 large aubergines
- 3 garlic cloves, thinly sliced and then cut into thin spikes
- 5 tablespoons olive oil
- 750ml sunflower oil
- 1 large fresh red chilli, seeded and cut into thin slivers
- 1 small bunch fresh mint leaves, roughly chopped
- sea salt and black pepper

DRESSING
- 1 garlic clove, crushed to a paste with salt
- 4 tablespoons red wine vinegar

Remove the stalks and cut each aubergine across widthways in slices about 2cm thick. Place in a colander, sprinkle liberally with salt and let them stand for about half an hour. Meanwhile, fry the garlic in the olive oil over a medium heat until golden brown. Remove and drain, keeping both garlic and oil (the latter to use again in another dish). Rinse the aubergines and pat dry. In a large saucepan heat the sunflower oil until it begins to smoke. Fry the aubergines in batches until dark brown on both sides. Remove and drain.

To assemble the salad, put one layer of aubergines in a dish (not over-lapping). Roughly estimating how much you will need per layer, sprinkle the dressing, fried garlic, chilli and mint over the top until all the ingredients have been used up. Let the aubergines sit for at least an hour or two to infuse.

Chard stalks with tahini

Sometimes when you buy chard, especially Swiss chard which has thick stalks, you may have more stalks than you need. This dish is a perfect way to use them up.

Serves 4
  500g chard stalks, washed and trimmed
  Tahini Sauce (see page 255)
  1 teaspoon nigella seeds (see page 40)
  sea salt

Bring a large saucepan of salted water to the boil. Add the chard stalks, put a lid on and wait for the water to come back to the boil. Cook for 30 seconds more and check to see if the stalks are tender. (Thicker stalks may require more time.) Drain in a colander and run under cold water for a short while to cool. Leave to drain. Slice stalks roughly 4cm long and 2cm thick. Toss with the tahini sauce and serve with a few nigella seeds on top.

Baba ghanoush

Baba ghanoush, or 'moutabel' as it is otherwise known, is a favourite on mezze tables throughout the Middle East, especially in the Lebanon, and when it is done well, you will understand why. The secret is to char the skins properly to impart a wonderful smoky flavour to the aubergines. A barbecue is ideal for this, but a hot grill or the flame of a gas hob also achieves good results. It is important to balance the smoky aubergine with the tahini, garlic and lemon so no one flavour is overbearing but all work in harmony with each other. The quantities below are guidelines, as it depends on the size of the aubergines, so taste is the best judge of all.

Serves 4-6

> 3 large aubergines, about 750g-1 kg in total
> 2 garlic cloves, crushed to a paste with 1 teaspoon salt
> juice of 1 lemon
> 3 tablespoons tahini paste (see page 186)
> 4 tablespoons olive oil
> sea salt and black pepper

Pierce the skins of the aubergines to prevent them from exploding and grill whole over a hot barbecue, directly on the naked flame of a gas hob, or under the grill until the skin is charred and crispy all over and the flesh is very soft. If none of these options is available, place in a very hot oven at 220°C/425°F/Gas 7 for about 45-60 minutes until soft inside. Remove from the heat.

When cool enough to handle, discard the tops and peel off the skin, scraping the flesh from the back of the skin if necessary. Place the flesh and any juices in a large mixing bowl and either whisk or beat by hand until almost smooth (we like a bit of texture). Add the garlic, lemon juice, tahini and olive oil, stir in and taste for seasoning. If the taste is a little strong, add a few tablespoons of water. When fresh pomegranates are in season (see page 283) scatter some seeds on top, and serve with lots of warm Flatbread (see page 18).

Tabbouleh

Most of us visualise tabbouleh as bulgur with specks of herbs, but in the Lebanon it is very green with specks of bulgur. At the restaurant we do something in between, still very herby, but with enough chewy bulgur. There are three subtle tips for this simple mineral tonic of a salad:

- For the right texture it is important to use flat-leaf parsley.
- Try not to bruise the herbs when chopping them, so always use a sharp knife or mezzaluna.
- When chopping the tomatoes, do so with care, for they must look jewel-like and not at all squashed.

Serves 4

85g fine bulgur wheat (see Lebanese and Turkish Suppliers)
400g sweetest tomatoes, seeded and cut into 5mm cubes
4 spring onions, trimmed and chopped
3 small bunches fresh flat-leaf parsley, roughly chopped
1 small bunch fresh mint, roughly chopped

DRESSING
1 garlic clove, crushed to a paste with salt
¼ teaspoon ground cinnamon
¼ teaspoon ground allspice
2 tablespoons lemon juice
3 tablespoons olive oil
sea salt and black pepper

With fine bulgur all you have to do is wash it well in a sieve and shake it dry; it will have absorbed enough water for it to swell. If you can only get medium bulgur it should sit in cold water for 3 minutes to swell before it is put in the sieve.

Mix all the salad ingredients together. To make the dressing we first like to add the garlic, salt and spices to the lemon juice (the flavours are more easily dispersed and dissolved) and then to stir in the olive oil. Toss the salad just before you are ready to eat and finally check for seasoning.

Falafel

Although considered Egyptian in origin, falafel are common throughout the Middle East. For a nuttier flavour, we like to use dried fava beans (see page 67), but chickpeas are just as good.

Serves 4

    250g dried fava beans, soaked overnight

    3 garlic cloves, crushed to a paste with salt

    1 large bunch fresh coriander, roughly chopped

    1 medium bunch fresh flat-leaf parsley, roughly chopped

    1½ teaspoons cumin seeds, roughly ground

    1 teaspoon coriander seeds, roughly ground

    ½ onion, grated

    50g chickpea flour or plain flour

    1 egg

    ¼ teaspoon bicarbonate of soda

    750ml sunflower oil for deep-frying

    4 tablespoons sesame seeds (optional)

    sea salt and black pepper

Drain the beans well and place half of them in a large saucepan. Fill with fresh cold water and bring to the boil. Reduce to a gentle simmer and cook for 5-10 minutes or until tender, skimming off any scum as it builds up. Meanwhile, place the raw beans in a food processor and pulse until more or less smooth. Transfer to a mixing bowl, and repeat the process for the cooked drained beans. Add the garlic, fresh coriander, parsley, cumin and coriander seeds, onion, flour, egg and bicarbonate of soda. Mix well and season with salt and black pepper to taste. Shape into balls no larger than a walnut, then gently flatten each one into a disc about 2cm thick, 5cm in diameter, making sure the edges do not crack. Place the sesame seeds on a plate and dip the falafel until coated all over.

    Heat the oil in a large saucepan and when the oil is hot but not smoking, add the falafel in batches. Fry until golden brown on both sides, remove and drain on kitchen paper. We serve falafel with Flatbread (see page 18), Tahini Sauce (see page 255), a wedge of lemon, some pickled chillies and sometimes with other mezze like Tabbouleh (see page 45).

Wilted herb salad

Wild herbs gathered in Morocco are the origin of this interesting dish.

Serves 4

> 1 bunch fresh mint, leaves picked from the stalks
>
> 2 large bunches fresh flat-leaf parsley, leaves picked from the stalks
>
> 2 large bunches fresh coriander, leaves and stalks
>
> 100g rocket
>
> 100g spinach, shredded
>
> 4 tablespoons olive oil
>
> 1 garlic clove, thinly sliced
>
> ¼ preserved lemon, rind only, washed and finely chopped (see
> Suppliers), or the zest and juice of ½ lemon (optional)
>
> Yoghurt and Cumin Sauce (see page 133)
>
> sea salt and black pepper

Roughly chop all the herbs and spinach together. Heat the oil in a large saucepan over a medium heat. Add the garlic and gently fry for a few seconds until it begins to colour. Immediately add the herbs and stir well. Continue to cook until the herbs wilt, then stir in the preserved lemon or lemon (if using) and taste for seasoning. Preserved lemons have quite a strong flavour and can be salty, so bear this in mind when you adjust the final seasoning. Wilted herb salad is good with Labneh, a strained yoghurt cheese (see page 51).

Pickled turnips

Pickles are an essential part of any mezze spread. At Moro we pickle turnips, but you can find almost every type of pickled vegetable in Lebanese and Turkish shops. The addition of beetroot in this recipe gives the turnips a vibrant purple hue.

Serves 4

    1 kg turnips (see method)
    1 raw large beetroot, peeled and sliced
    approx. 400ml red wine vinegar (or pickling vinegar)
    approx. 1 litre water
    1 teaspoon allspice berries
    1 teaspoon whole black peppercorns
    4-5 tablespoons sea salt
    8 garlic cloves, peeled

We like to pickle whole baby turnips, but large sizes work just as well and are more common. If the turnips are baby-sized, keep whole, trim both ends and wash thoroughly; if the size of a tangerine, peel and quarter. It is very important to clean the turnips and to sterilise the jar thoroughly to prevent bacteria from spoiling the turnips. Place the vinegar, water, allspice and peppercorns in a saucepan and heat for a few minutes to help infuse the flavours. Dissolve the salt and taste for seasoning. The amount of salt you will need depends on the acidity of the vinegar and your personal taste, so adjust with more salt or water accordingly. Allow to cool completely. Place the turnips in the jar, and intermittently layer with the beetroot and garlic. Fill with the vinegar-water solution, cover generously and seal the lid so it is airtight. Store in a warm place. The turnips will be ready in about a week to ten days and once opened should be kept in the fridge for a good three to four weeks.

Laban

YOGHURT

Yoghurt can be traced back as far as 10,000 BC, and its origins lie in the Muslim Mediterranean. Like bread, its value has been recognised amongst both ancient and modern civilisations as an important food source, and for its restorative, healthy qualities. We use yoghurt a lot in the restaurant for our Muslim Mediterranean recipes, especially ones from Turkey, Lebanon and Syria, although interestingly it does not feature in the North African diet.

Yoghurt is a living thing, a culture, like the sourdough starter for our bread. At Moro, we always make our own yoghurt, saving some from the old batch to make a new batch. Making yoghurt is a satisfying and easy process, but if you do not have time, we recommend you use Greek yoghurt thinned with a little milk. This recipe will yield just over 1 kg yoghurt.

2 litres full-fat milk
300ml double cream
150g live yoghurt (approx. 4 tablespoons)

Place the milk in a large saucepan, making sure the pan is no more than two-thirds full. Bring to the boil, stirring often to prevent the milk sticking to the bottom of the pan (otherwise it may burn and give a smoky flavour). Turn down the heat to a gentle simmer and reduce by a third, again stirring occasionally. Remove the pan from the heat and transfer the milk to a ceramic or stainless-steel bowl. Add the cream and stir well. Allow to cool. When you are able to hold your finger in the milk and count to ten, add the yoghurt and stir well. If the milk is too hot when the live yoghurt culture is added, the bacteria may be killed. If it is not hot enough, it will take a lot longer to set. Cover with clingfilm and leave to stand in a warm place (an airing cupboard is ideal), wrapped in a cloth if possible, for about 8 hours or overnight, until set. Yoghurt keeps in the fridge for seven to ten days.

Labneh
YOGHURT CHEESE

Labneh is yoghurt that has been strained into cheese, and is a great feature on many mezze tables throughout the Muslim Mediterranean. It is usually served with an array of raw vegetables (carrots, celery, radish, tomato and cucumber) as well as bunches of fresh herbs (mint and tarragon especially), olives and pickles.

1 kg home-made or Greek yoghurt
approx. 1 teaspoon fine sea salt

Pour the yoghurt into a mixing bowl, add the salt and stir well. The amount of salt you need will depend on the acidity of the yoghurt, but just as long as you can taste it. Line a narrow bowl with a muslin cloth or fine cloth and spoon the yoghurt into the centre. Draw up the corners of the cloth and tie together with string or an elastic band. Suspend over a suitable place, either over the sink or over a bowl, and leave overnight or longer if necessary. The labneh will vary in thickness depending on how long you strain it for. The consistency of a thick mayonnaise is a good guide. Keep in the fridge until ready to use or spread on a plate and drizzle with olive oil. Scoop up with warm Flatbread (see page 18).

LABNEH BALLS

If you strain the labneh for a further 24–36 hours, its consistency should be thick enough to shape it into small balls. Lay these on a tray and place in the fridge, uncovered, for 12 hours more to dry out. Then roll them in spices (cumin or paprika) or herbs (thyme or oregano) and put in a sealable jar and cover them with olive oil. They will keep for two months in the fridge, but be sure to bring them up to room temperature before you eat them.

SPICED LABNEH

To make Labneh, see the previous page, or use two parts Greek or home-made yoghurt to one part cream cheese. The fenugreek in this recipe gives this labneh an original taste.

Serves 4-6

$1\frac{1}{2}$ teaspoons whole fenugreek seeds

approx. 500g Labneh (see page 51)

1 garlic clove, crushed to a paste with salt

2 large fresh green chillies, halved lengthways, seeded and finely chopped

1 dessertspoon nigella seeds (see page 40)

olive oil

sea salt and black pepper

Pour boiling water over the fenugreek seeds and leave to soak for a couple of hours, changing the water a couple of times, until the seeds are soft and have lost some of their bitter taste. Drain and set aside. Place the labneh into a bowl with the garlic, fenugreek, chilli and half the nigella seeds, and mix well. Season with salt and pepper and spread out on a large plate. Sprinkle the remaining seeds on top and drizzle with a little olive oil.

In the restaurant we sometimes serve this dish with sprouted fenu-greek seeds. Simply place 2 tablespoons of the seeds in a jam jar with the same amount of warm water. Puncture the lid or secure the top with a piece of cloth and an elastic band to allow them to breathe a little. Give the jar a good shake and put in a warm place – the airing cupboard is ideal. Check after 24 hours. When the seeds begin to sprout, they might need a little more water. They are ready to eat when the shoots are about 3cm long (this can take up to two to three days).

SOUPS

On our travels we have tasted a wonderfully varied selection of soups, ranging from elegant and refreshing to restorative and warming, and many of these have become the mainstay of Moro's repertoire. Each one is a snapshot of a region, revealing something of its culture and resources. We like to think that in making one of these soups it is possible to recreate the essence of a region's food.

Gazpacho

In the same way that the almond soup 'ajo blanco' is a legacy of the Moors, gazpacho is a legacy of the New World when Columbus returned from his travels with tomatoes and peppers. Gazpacho is a soup that many people will be vaguely familiar with, but few people will have tasted it at its best. For us a memorable gazpacho has to be made when it is hot. Hot when the tomatoes are sweet, ripe and bursting with flavour. Hot when its refreshing deliciousness is a joy. A thicker version of gazpacho called 'salmorejo' comes from Córdoba and is served with bits of jamón (cured ham) and chopped egg. Sometimes we serve gazpacho with chopped tomato, pepper and onion, and sometimes we keep it pure; it is up to you.

Serves 4

>   3 garlic cloves
>   1 kg sweet tomatoes, halved
>   1 green pepper, seeded, cored and sliced
>   ¾ cucumber, peeled and sliced
>   2 rounded dessertspoons finely grated onion
>   2 handfuls slightly stale white bread, with crusts removed, roughly
>   crumbled
>   3 dessertspoons good-quality red wine vinegar or sherry vinegar
>   (See Suppliers. At Moro we use a slightly sweet Spanish Cabernet
>   Sauvignon vinegar.)
>   4 dessertspoons olive oil
>   sea salt and black pepper

Crush the garlic in a mortar and pestle with a good pinch of salt until you have a smooth paste. Using a blender or food processor, purée all the vegetables and the bread until smooth. Now put three-quarters of the mixture through a sieve or mouli, to give a finer texture. Finish by seasoning the soup with the garlic, vinegar, oil, salt and black pepper. If you want a thinner or lighter soup add four ice cubes. (For a creamier version, also blend in hard-boiled egg yolk.) Now put in the fridge for 2 hours to cool. It is always advisable to check the balance of the vinegar and seasoning once the soup is cold.

Almendras
ALMONDS

 The almond is a key ingredient of the Spanish diet, and probably the most versatile as it features in every aspect of Spanish cooking, from tapas to soups, sauces to stews, and from puddings to sweets. The word for almond – 'almendra' – has roots in the Moorish past, for the Arabs were very partial to them and planted trees all along the Mediterranean coast from Tarragona to Málaga. When the trees flower in late winter there is a spectacular blaze of white and pink blossom; the fruit are harvested in August and September. (See Spanish Suppliers)

Ajo blanco
WHITE GAZPACHO

This ancient and classic Spanish chilled soup comes from Málaga. The recipe is a culinary legacy of the Moors, who adored almonds, the soup's main ingredient. Ajo blanco is usually served with grapes, or sometimes with raisins and apple or melon. Traditionally the ingredients are pounded together in a mortar and pestle, but a food processor works very well. At Moro, we use sherry vinegar instead of white wine vinegar for a more complex flavour.

Serves 4

> 225g whole blanched almonds, preferably Spanish (see above)
> 750ml iced water
> 75g stale white bread, with crusts removed, soaked in water
> 3 garlic cloves, crushed to a paste with 1 level teaspoon sea salt
> 3 tablespoons olive oil
> 3 tablespoons sherry vinegar
> 200g white grapes, preferably Moscatel (Muscat)
> sea salt and black pepper

In a food processor, grind the almonds until the consistency is as fine as possible. At this point they should stick to the side of the machine. Turn off and loosen the nuts from around the edge. Add 5 tablespoons of the iced water. Turn the machine back on until the almonds form a paste just fluid enough to turn in on itself. Squeeze the bread of excess water and add to the almonds along with the garlic. Combine until smooth. Add the olive oil and gradually pour in the rest of the iced water, until you end up with a very smooth paste similar to single cream. Transfer to a bowl and season with sherry vinegar and salt to taste. You should end up with a nice balance between the almonds, garlic and sherry vinegar. Chill the soup for at least an hour. Just before serving, check for seasoning again. Ladle into bowls and distribute the grapes evenly. Perfect for a fine summer's day.

Sopa de picadillo
JAMON BROTH WITH FINO

The secret of this Andalucían soup is a really good meat stock, traditionally made from the broth of a 'cocido' or 'puchero', the classic Spanish dish of boiled meats and vegetables. In the restaurant we simmer a jamón bone in the stock, but as this is impractical at home, gently simmer slices of jamón (cured ham) to impart some of its sweet, salty flavour. The 'picadillo' or garnish adds colour and vitality to make this broth clean and restorative.

Serves 4

     100g thinly sliced jamón serrano (cured ham), roughly chopped (see page 116)

     1.25 litres good Chicken Stock (see page 175), unseasoned

     3 tablespoons fino sherry (see Sherry Suppliers)

     sea salt and black pepper

PICADILLO

     75g white rice or rice pasta, cooked in water or stock and drained

     1 hard-boiled egg, chopped

     ½ small bunch fresh mint, roughly chopped

     50g thinly sliced jamón, finely chopped

Gently simmer the 100g jamón in the stock for 10–15 minutes until the flavour has been released. Discard the jamón, add the sherry, and season with a little black pepper (the stock may be salty enough).

To serve, add the rice, egg, mint and remaining jamón to the hot broth and taste for seasoning once more.

Sopa de setas

MUSHROOM AND ALMOND SOUP WITH FINO

The 'flor' (fungus) that lives with fino sherry in the barrel, and gives fino much of its musty character, complements mushrooms wonderfully. The almonds in this recipe give richness and texture to the soup.

Serves 4

      4 tablespoons olive oil

      1 large onion, finely chopped

      3 garlic cloves, thinly sliced

      ¾ teaspoon fresh thyme leaves

      250g mushrooms (flat field or a mixture of field and wild like chanterelles or pied de mouton), finely chopped

      1 litre Chicken Stock (see page 175) or water

      5 tablespoons fino sherry

      1½ dessertspoons dried porcini mushrooms, covered with boiling water to infuse

      130g blanched almonds, lightly toasted

      1 small bunch fresh flat-leaf parsley, roughly chopped

      sea salt and black pepper

Heat the oil in a saucepan and over a medium heat, soften the onion and garlic for 15-20 minutes until golden and sweet, stirring every now and then. Add the thyme and fresh mushrooms and cook for another 15 minutes or until the moisture in the mushrooms has evaporated. Season with salt and pepper. Now add your stock or water, fino and chopped dried porcini and their juice to the pan. Bring to the boil and simmer for 5 minutes.

Meanwhile pound the almonds in small batches in a mortar and pestle or in a blender until as fine as possible. Stir the almonds and parsley into the soup, taste for seasoning once more, and serve.

Sopa de guisantes

PEA SOUP WITH JAMON AND MINT

Peas with jamón (cured ham) is a classic combination in Spain. We particularly like this soup for its emerald colour and its sweet flavour that complements the salty tang of the jamón.

Serves 4

>   4 tablespoons olive oil
>   ½ medium onion, finely chopped
>   1 medium carrot, finely chopped
>   2 bay leaves, preferably fresh
>   2 garlic cloves, thinly sliced
>   150g jamón serrano (cured ham), finely chopped (see page 116)
>   1 small bunch fresh mint, roughly chopped
>   500g podded peas, fresh or frozen
>   1 litre Chicken Stock (see page 175, and if using fresh peas, add the pods to the stock for extra flavour)
>   sea salt and black pepper

In a large saucepan, heat the oil over a medium heat, add the onion, and when it has turned golden add the carrot and bay leaves. Continue to fry for about 5 minutes, stirring occasionally, then add the garlic, two-thirds of the jamón and half the mint. Give everything a good stir, fry for another minute or so, then add the peas. Cook for a couple of minutes before adding the stock. Simmer gently until the peas are tender, about 2-3 minutes. Remove from the heat. Ladle the peas and stock into a food processor or liquidiser, and process until smooth. Return to the pan, season with salt and pepper and add the remaining mint. Serve with the rest of the jamón on top and an extra drizzle of olive oil.

Sopa de castañas
CHESTNUT AND CHORIZO SOUP

Forests of sweet chestnut thrive in the mountainous regions of Spain. This recipe combines some of the classic flavours of Spanish cooking to produce a warm, comforting and mildly spicy soup that is synonymous with the onset of autumn.

Serves 4

      4 tablespoons olive oil

      1 large Spanish onion, diced

      1 medium carrot, diced

      1 celery stick, thinly sliced

      120g mild cooking chorizo, cut into 1cm cubes

      2 garlic cloves, thinly sliced

      1 teaspoon ground cumin

      1½ teaspoons finely chopped fresh thyme leaves

      2 small dried red chillies, crushed

      2 tomatoes, fresh or tinned, roughly chopped

      500g cooked peeled chestnuts (fresh or vacuum-packed), roughly chopped

      20 saffron threads, infused in 3-4 tablespoons boiling water

      1 litre water

      sea salt and black pepper

In a large saucepan heat the oil over a medium heat. Add the onion, carrot, celery, chorizo and a pinch of salt and fry for about 20 minutes, stirring occasionally, until everything caramelises and turns quite brown. This gives the soup a wonderfully rich colour and taste. Now add the garlic, cumin, thyme and chilli and cook for 1 more minute, followed by the tomato and, after about 2 minutes, the chestnuts. Give everything a good stir, then add the saffron-infused liquid, and the water, and simmer for about 10 minutes. Remove from the heat and mash by hand (with a potato masher) until almost smooth but still with a little bit of texture. Season with salt and pepper.

Sopa de ajo
GARLIC SOUP

Velásquez's painting, 'Old Lady Cooking Eggs', which hangs in the National Gallery of Scotland, is readily conjured up when we make this soup. Despite regional variations, the main ingredients always remain the same: garlic, eggs, bread and paprika. But do not be misled by what you might consider simple and perhaps unexciting elements, for this noble and sustaining soup is a classic throughout Spain, especially in Castilla-La Mancha. We tasted this version in a famous restaurant called Mesón de Cándido, in Segovia.

Serves 4

    4 tablespoons olive oil

    4-5 large garlic bulbs, broken into cloves with skin kept on

    100g cooking chorizo, cut into little pieces

    1 teaspoon fresh thyme leaves

    ½ teaspoon sweet smoked Spanish paprika (see page 111)

    1 litre good Chicken Stock (see page 175)

    4 eggs, organic or free-range

    8 slices ciabatta or 4 slices Moro Sourdough (see page 14), toasted
        and torn into rough pieces

    sea salt and black pepper

Heat the oil in a saucepan over a low flame and add the garlic. Gently fry for 15-20 minutes, stirring often, until the skins are golden brown but not dark, and the flesh inside is soft. Remove with a slotted spoon. When slightly cool, squeeze out the sweet garlic flesh by hand (discarding the skins), purée and set aside. Meanwhile, add the chorizo to the pan and fry until crisp and caramelised. Add the thyme, fry for a few seconds, then the puréed garlic. Stir well, add the paprika and finally pour on the chicken stock. Bring to a gentle simmer and check for seasoning. About 2 minutes before serving, poach the eggs in the soup and add the toasted bread. Taste once more and serve immediately. This hearty soup is perfect for a cold winter's day.

Sopa de pescado
FISH SOUP WITH BRANDY

If you ever buy a whole fish and fillet it yourself, don't throw away the head as you can transform scraps destined for the bin into a soup fit for kings. This rich and lightly spiced soup comes from a Basque chef, Alvaro, who worked for us at Moro.

Serves 4

> 5 tablespoons olive oil
> 1 large Spanish onion, diced
> 1 medium carrot, diced
> 1 large bunch fresh flat-leaf parsley, roughly chopped
> 3 garlic cloves, sliced
> 2 small dried red chillies, crushed
> 2 bay leaves, preferably fresh
> 1 or 2 fish heads (total weight, 1 kg), with gills removed (turbot, sea
>   bass or cod are best, ask your fishmonger)
> 200ml brandy, preferably Spanish
> 150ml red wine
> 2 x 400g tins plum tomatoes, strained of juice, roughly chopped
> 1 teaspoon sweet smoked Spanish paprika (see page 111)
> sea salt and black pepper

Place a large saucepan over a medium heat and add the olive oil. When hot, add the onion and fry until translucent. Now add the carrot, parsley stalks, garlic, chilli and bay leaves and stir well. When everything begins to colour, add the fish head and cook for 10 minutes, stirring occasionally. Add the brandy and red wine and reduce for about 3 minutes to burn off the alcohol. Now stir in the tomatoes, paprika and season with salt and pepper. When the juice has more or less evaporated, cover with water and simmer for 5–10 more minutes. Remove from the heat, strain the liquid and return it to the pan. Liquidise the head with some of the stock either in a mouli or food processor and add the pulp back to the pan, discarding any bones that have not been blended. This will give the soup its goodness and texture, but if very thick, add a little water. Return to the heat, season with more salt and pepper and stir in the chopped parsley leaves. Sometimes we serve this soup with a few croûtons for crunch.

Potato, cucumber and fava bean soup

This is one of our favourite soups, which is Lebanese in origin. Fava beans are dried, skinned broad beans that have a nutty flavour. This soup can be enjoyed at room temperature in summer or warm. If you cannot source fava beans, simply make a potato and cucumber soup, using 4–5 medium potatoes (about 900g).

Serves 4

200g dried fava beans (see Lebanese and Turkish Suppliers)
5 tablespoons olive oil
½ large Spanish onion, thinly sliced
2 garlic cloves, thinly sliced
1 teaspoon black cumin seeds (see page 72) or caraway seeds
2 medium potatoes, diced and lightly salted
4 tablespoons chopped fresh dill, leaves and stalks
1 large cucumber, washed, skin peeled in strips, half on, half off
100g home-made or Greek yoghurt, thinned with a little milk and
    seasoned with 1 garlic clove crushed to a paste with salt
sea salt and black pepper

Rinse the fava beans well and place in a large saucepan. Fill with 2 litres cold water and bring to a gentle simmer, skimming off any scum, and cook for 20 minutes or until tender. Drain and reserve 500ml of the liquid. Meanwhile, in a large saucepan, heat the oil. Add the onion and a pinch of salt, and cook for about 10 minutes, stirring occasionally, until the onion is sweet and golden. Now add the garlic and cumin or caraway and fry for 2 more minutes, followed by the potatoes and half the dill. Cook for 2 minutes. Now add the reserved fava bean liquid, a further 400–500ml water (or 900ml if using just potatoes), and simmer until the potatoes are soft. Add the fava, then mash by hand or process until almost smooth. Return to the pan and check for seasoning. Just before you are ready to serve, coarsely grate the cucumber and stir into the soup along with the rest of the dill. It is important there is a high proportion of cucumber as this makes the soup fresh and light. Spoon the yoghurt on top along with an extra drizzle of olive oil.

Lebanese spring vegetable soup

As the first broad beans, peas and asparagus arrive in the market in spring, we always celebrate by making this fresh soup. This was one of the first soups we served at the restaurant and it immediately became a classic.

Serves 4

Crispbread (see page 146)

1 litre Chicken Stock (see page 175)

150g podded young broad beans (peeled if large)

150g shelled peas, fresh or frozen

5 green asparagus spears, woody stems snapped off at base,
cut into 2cm pieces (keep tips intact)

2 raw globe artichokes, trimmed (see page 122), cut into quarters and
very thinly sliced

1 large bunch each of roughly chopped fresh mint, flat-leaf
parsley and coriander

2 spring onions, finely chopped

juice of ½ lemon

sea salt and black pepper

When the crispbread is ready, heat the chicken stock in a large saucepan and check for seasoning. Bring to a gentle simmer and add the broad beans, peas, asparagus and artichokes. Cook for 1–2 minutes until the vegetables are tender. Remove from the heat and add the herbs, spring onion, lemon juice and crispbread broken into small pieces. Season again, and serve hot.

Caramelised butter

Caramelised butter is regularly used in Turkish cooking, often twinned with yoghurt. The combination is simple yet magical. To serve four, place 75g unsalted butter in a small saucepan and set over the lowest heat. As the butter melts, the whey will separate. Continue to heat gently, stirring occasionally, until the white bits turn golden brown. This gives the butter a wonderfully nutty, caramelised aroma, but be careful the bits do not get too dark as they will burn easily.

Leek and yoghurt soup
with dried mint

Yoghurt soups are common throughout the eastern Mediterranean, especially in Turkey, and they generally vary according to what is in season. In this recipe, the tartness of the yoghurt is balanced by the sweetness of the caramelised leeks.

Serves 4

      50g butter

      3 tablespoons olive oil

      4 medium leeks, trimmed, cut in half lengthways, washed, drained, and thinly sliced

      1 teaspoon Turkish chilli flakes (see Turkish Suppliers) or paprika

      1 rounded teaspoon dried mint

      1 egg

      ½ tablespoon plain flour

      350g home-made or Greek yoghurt

      500ml water or Chicken Stock (see page 175)

      Caramelised Butter (see above)

      sea salt and black pepper

Place a large saucepan over a medium heat and add the butter and olive oil. When the butter begins to foam, stir in the leeks. After 10 minutes add the chilli flakes or paprika and dried mint, and continue to cook the leeks for another 20–30 minutes, stirring occasionally until they are sweet. Set aside.

In a large bowl, whisk the egg with the flour until a smooth paste is formed. This will stabilise the yoghurt when it is heated. Now stir in the yoghurt and thin with the water or stock. Pour on to the leeks and return the saucepan to the heat. Gently heat the soup over a low to medium heat, stirring every now and then. Do not allow the soup to boil, but remove from the heat just before it bubbles. The soup should have a smooth, silky quality, about the consistency of single cream. Check for seasoning and pour the caramelised butter on top.

VARIATION: When wild garlic leaves are in season, substitute them for leeks. Sauté in olive oil until sweet and tender, chop finely and add to the soup along with 75g cooked white rice.

Beetroot soup with black cumin

This simple soup is similar to borscht but with a hint of spice. The black cumin gives it an ethereal quality, which takes it to a new height. This is a rare variety of cumin that has more of an aromatic nutty flavour than normal cumin; the seeds are finer and more curled in shape. It is usually found in Indian/Bengali shops under the name of 'kala jeerd'. This soup is also delicious made with sherry vinegar instead of red wine vinegar, but omit the cumin and yoghurt.

Serves 4

> 4 tablespoons olive oil
> ½ large Spanish onion, thinly sliced
> 2 garlic cloves, thinly sliced
> 1 rounded teaspoon black cumin or normal cumin seeds
> 750g raw beetroot, peeled and finely diced
> 1 large potato, finely diced
> 1.25 litres cold water
> 3 tablespoons good-quality red wine vinegar
> 1 small bunch fresh flat-leaf parsley, roughly chopped
> 100g home-made or Greek yoghurt, thinned with a little milk and
>   seasoned with 1 garlic clove crushed to a paste with salt
> sea salt and black pepper

Heat the oil in a large saucepan over a medium heat. Add the onion and a pinch of salt. Cook for 10 minutes, stirring occasionally, until the onion begins to colour. Now add the garlic and cumin and cook for 2 more minutes to release their flavour, followed by the beetroot and potato. Pour in the water, bring to a gentle simmer and cook until soft, about 15 minutes. Place the vegetables and the cooking liquid in a blender or food processor and blend until just smooth. You may need to do this in two stages. Return to the pan, add the vinegar, half the parsley, and salt and pepper to taste, bearing in mind you may need more salt than you think to balance out the acidity of the vinegar. Serve with a little yoghurt on top, the rest of the parsley and an extra drizzle of olive oil.

Harira

We always imagine the name of this soup being spoken with a guttural Islamic tongue, and being eaten without ceremony at the edge of a busy bus station somewhere in Morocco. The flavours of the spices and coriander are very evocative, and only the bus fumes are missing. On reflection the best hariras we have tasted have had a slightly sour taste, given either by slightly fermented flour or lemon juice.

Serves 4

 350g neck of lamb in 3 or 4 pieces, or shank
 2 litres cold water
 1 large onion, finely chopped
 3 garlic cloves, finely chopped
 3 celery sticks, finely chopped
 a pinch of saffron strands
 ½ teaspoon ground cinnamon
 ½ teaspoon turmeric
 ¾ teaspoon ground ginger
 nutmeg (5 grates on a fine grater)
 2 large bunches fresh coriander, washed and chopped
 100g small green lentils
 120g chana dhal (small, split and skinned chickpeas)
 1 dessertspoon tomato purée
 3 rounded dessertspoons plain flour or fine semolina flour,
   slaked in 50ml water
 juice of 1 lemon
 50g unsalted butter (optional)
 1 lemon, quartered
 sea salt and black pepper

Put the neck of lamb into a large saucepan with the water. Bring to the boil and simmer for 5 minutes, skimming off any scum or fat as it appears. Add the onion, garlic, celery, saffron, cinnamon, turmeric, ginger, nutmeg, salt and pepper as well as half the coriander. Cook for half an hour before adding the lentils and chana dhal, then simmer for another half-hour. Take out the pieces of lamb. The lamb should now be soft enough to be pulled off the bone and flaked a little. Return the lamb meat to the pot, along with the tomato purée, flour mixture and lemon juice. Season the soup with salt (because of the lemon juice this soup may need more salt than one would expect). Continue to cook for 10 minutes, or until the pulses are soft. Take off the heat, and stir in the butter and the remaining coriander. Serve with a wedge of lemon and, if you're feeling exotic, sweet dates at the side.

Fish soup with dried limes

We have always greatly admired Iranian food, and dried limes are a signature ingredient. We make this soup purely as a vehicle for the intriguing musty, slightly sour flavour of the limes, and it has proved very popular.

Serves 4

>   4 tablespoons olive oil
>   1 large Spanish onion, finely chopped
>   2 celery sticks, sliced
>   4 garlic cloves, finely chopped
>   ¾ teaspoon turmeric
>   1–2 dried limes, seeded, crushed and ground (see Iranian Suppliers)
>   1 x 400g tin plum tomatoes, broken up in the juice and any hard bits
>   removed
>   1 litre Fish Stock (see page 175)
>   1 teaspoon caster sugar
>   250g skinned white fish fillet, cut in 1cm slices
>   2 tablespoons roughly chopped fresh flat-leaf parsley
>   sea salt and black pepper

Heat the olive oil in a saucepan and soften the onion, celery and garlic for 15-20 minutes until sweet. Stir in the turmeric and dried limes, cook for 1 minute, then add the tomatoes and continue to cook for a further 20 minutes. Add the fish stock, bring to the boil and season with salt and pepper and the sugar. Stir in the fish and parsley, simmer for 1 minute to poach the fish, then serve.

Lentil soup with cumin

The first meal we ate on Moroccan soil was lentil soup. We had just taken the ferry from Algeciras to Tangiers and had arrived slightly weary and hungry from the day's travelling. We soon stumbled across a dark room filled with a few tables and a few people who kept one eye on their food, the other on us. There was only one thing on offer – lentil soup. We sat down and were immediately presented with a bowl of this steaming soup, a dish of harissa, some juicy, oily black olives and a couple of rounds of Moroccan bread. The soup was made from lentils subtly flavoured with cumin. It was a great introduction to Moroccan food: simple, exotically spiced and very satisfying, just what we felt like eating. We make this soup in the restaurant and sometimes add spinach for variety.

Serves 4

    4 tablespoons olive oil
    ½ large Spanish onion, thinly sliced
    4 garlic cloves, thinly sliced
    1½ rounded teaspoons cumin seeds, roughly ground
    250g lentils (brown, green or yellow)
    1.75 litres cold water
    250g spinach braised with olive oil (see page 234), roughly chopped
    1 lemon, quartered, or 150g yoghurt spiced with ¾ teaspoon
        ground cumin and salt
    sea salt and black pepper

In a large saucepan, heat the oil over a medium heat. Add the onion with a pinch of salt and cook for about 10 minutes, stirring occasionally, until sweet and golden. Now add the garlic and cumin and fry for another minute, followed by the lentils and water. Bring to the boil, reduce the heat to a gentle simmer, and cook for about 20 minutes or until the lentils are soft. Remove from the heat and blend all the ingredients either in a food processor or by hand until almost smooth. Return to the pan along with the spinach, and season with salt and pepper. If the soup is too thick, simply add more water and adjust the seasoning. We serve this soup with lemon or yoghurt, and olives, Harissa (see page 254) and Moroccan bread (see page 20).

FISH STARTERS

Many of the recipes in this chapter – and indeed in the chapters on meat and vegetable starters – originate from classic tapas or mezze that we have tasted on our travels. Back home at Moro, partly not wanting to keep some of these magical combinations just for the tapas board, and partly through the necessity of adapting them for a restaurant, we have evolved an exciting array of starters that constitute some of our best dishes.

For us, one of the great pleasures of the Mediterranean is that wherever you go you are never far away from some of the best fish markets in the world. Spain in particular benefits from being surrounded by water – the Mediterranean, the North Atlantic and the Bay of Biscay – and because of this, and the Spaniards' passion for seafood, it is easy to eat fish of unparalleled freshness and variety. We had one very memorable meal when we drove to Sanlúcar de Barrameda on the Atlantic coast of Andalucía. It was a Sunday, three o'clock in the afternoon and our restaurant, Casa Bigote, was buzzing, for Sunday lunch is one of the busiest times of the week. We sat down and ordered a half bottle of manzanilla, the sherry of the town, and a few things to eat. 'Gambas a la plancha' came first, pale pink prawns lightly grilled with rock salt, and were some of the sweetest, juiciest prawns we have ever tasted – every mouthful sent shivers of pleasure down our spines. After further plates of 'pijotas', deep-fried baby hakes, and some 'chipirones', baby squid – and more sherry – we left reeling from that rare and heady experience of all-consuming pleasure. Hand in hand with such a variety of seafood come so many recipes, so many ways of preparing, cooking and eating fish, that we could fill a whole book with what we have tasted, but below are some of our favourite dishes.

Mejillones a la vinagreta
MUSSELS VINAIGRETTE

We ate this particular dish in a small tapas bar in Madrid, but we have also eaten something similar with mixed shellfish called 'salpicón de mariscos'.

Serves 4

> 40–50 live mussels
> 100ml white wine or water
> 1 lemon, quartered

SALPICON (chopped salad)
> 15 cherry tomatoes (approx. 225g), halved and very finely diced
> ½ red onion, finely diced
> 1 green and 1 red pepper, seeded and finely diced
> 1 large bunch fresh flat-leaf parsley, roughly chopped

DRESSING
> 1 garlic clove, crushed to a paste with salt
> 2 tablespoons good-quality red wine vinegar
> 4 tablespoons extra-virgin olive oil
> sea salt and black pepper

Wash the mussels under cold water, getting rid of any beard or barnacles, and discard any open or broken shells. Set a large saucepan over a high heat and add the wine or water. When simmering, add the mussels and put the lid on. Cook for 2–3 minutes, shaking the pan until the mussels steam open. Remove and strain in a colander. Keep aside half the cooking liquid and discard any mussels that have not opened.

While the mussels are cooling, make the dressing. Whisk the garlic, vinegar, olive oil, and the mussel liquor together and taste for seasoning. Add the tomato, onion, peppers and parsley and chill for half an hour.

To serve, straighten out each mussel shell, and break off the meatless half. Lay on a large plate. Spoon the chilled mixture over the mussels. Serve immediately for room temperature, or place in the fridge for another half-hour for chilled, but always offer lemon on the side and good bread for mopping up the juices. Salpicón can also be mixed with chopped hard-boiled egg, capers or jamón (cured ham).

Tortillitas de camarones
SHRIMP OR PRAWN TORTILLITAS

When we asked what sort of shrimps were used for these, our host said, 'I don't know what they are called, but they must be alive.' The next day we did a double-take at a lady sitting outside Jerez fish market. Her basket's inhabitants were jiggling and jumping, and sure enough they were the live shrimps, 'camarones', for sale. Jumping shrimps aside, this is one of our most loved things to eat. They are crispy and lace-like, with a taste of the sea.

Serves 4

    200g peeled brown shrimps, or 300g prawns in their shells,
        peeled and thinly sliced
    approx. 200ml olive oil for shallow-frying
    1 lemon, quartered

    BATTER
    55g chickpea or gram flour (available from Indian shops)
    130ml soda water or water
    $\frac{1}{3}$ teaspoon sweet smoked Spanish paprika (see page 111)
    a pinch of bicarbonate of soda
    sea salt

To make the batter, sift the flour into a bowl and slowly add the soda water, mixing in with your fingertips or a wooden spoon, trying to avoid lumps forming. The batter should have the consistency of something between single and double cream. Add the paprika, bicarbonate of soda and salt to taste. Chill the batter, covered, for at least 20 minutes.

When ready to eat, stir your shrimps or sliced prawns into the batter. Pour enough oil into a large frying pan to cover the bottom liberally. Heat the oil to a medium to high temperature for about 3 minutes. Now with a dessertspoon scoop up a heaped spoonful of the mixture, carefully pour it into the oil and gently and quickly spread it out with the back of the spoon. Create two or three more tortillitas (depending on the size of the pan) in exactly the same way. When your first batch reaches a beautiful light brown colour, carefully turn over using a metal spatula and fork. Finish cooking the other side. Do this with all the mixture, lifting each tortillita out on to kitchen paper when ready. Serve immediately with some lemon on the side.

Deep-fried mussels with tarator

One of the stands in the covered market in Istanbul specialises in this classic Turkish mezze. Wooden skewers of plump, juicy mussels are first dredged in flour, then dipped in a light batter and immersed in a large vat of bubbling oil. The mussels sizzle for a couple of minutes until golden brown, and are served immediately with the garlicky tarator and lemon. Some people use beer instead of soda water to make the batter. You will need eight small wooden skewers, about 15cm long, or four long (30cm), cut in half.

Serves 4

    40-50 large mussels, washed, beard and barnacles removed and any
        open or broken shells discarded
    750ml sunflower oil for deep-frying
    6 tablespoons plain flour seasoned with salt and pepper
    Tarator (see page 256)
    1 lemon, quartered

    BATTER
    125g plain flour
    200ml soda water or beer
    a pinch of sea salt

To make the batter, sift the flour into a medium-sized bowl and make a well in the centre. Pour in the soda water or beer, and with a balloon whisk gradually draw the flour into the centre and stir until the flour and water are mixed thoroughly and there are no lumps. The batter should have the consistency of double cream. Rest the batter for at least an hour (this can be done ahead of time).

While the batter is resting, cook the mussels. Set a large pan over a high heat and pour in enough water just to cover the bottom of the pan. When the water comes to the boil add the mussels and steam until the shells begin to open. Remove from the heat and drain. Gently prise the flesh away from the shell and discard the shell. Thread five mussels on each skewer (two skewers per portion).

When you are ready to fry the mussels, heat the oil in a large saucepan (never more than half full). When the oil is hot but not smoking – test with a drop of batter – dust the skewers in the flour, shaking off any excess. Then dip in the batter, coat well and gently drop into the hot oil. Fry until golden, remove, drain on some kitchen paper and sprinkle with salt. Serve immediately with the tarator and lemon.

Bacalao
SALT COD

Being a predominantly North Atlantic fish, fresh cod or 'bacalao' rarely features in fish markets around Spain; however, the cured version, salt cod, also known as bacalao, is a different matter entirely. There are market stalls entirely dedicated to salt cod, selling different cuts and cures for different dishes, some at varying degrees of soaking, even a selection of classic recipes already prepared for you to take home. This Spanish and indeed Portuguese affection for salt cod (the Portuguese boast a different salt cod dish for every day of the year) dates back to the fifteenth century when cod was fished off the shores of North America, cured and brought to Europe. Salt cod has a distinctive smell, taste and sticky texture, which make it unique and, along with hake, is one of Spain's most popular fish.

HOW TO SOAK SALT COD
First wash the cod well under cold water to remove the dried salt. Then place in a large bowl skin-side up and cover with as much water as possible. Refrigerate and leave to soak, generally for about 24–48 hours depending on the cure, thickness of the cut, and recipe, changing the water about three to four times. As a general rule, when we cook the cod, it requires only about 24 hours' soaking but recipes using raw salt cod require more time, about 48 hours. In any case, always taste the soaked cod before you use it.

Esqueixada
SHREDDED SALT COD SALAD

'Esqueixada' is a refreshing and delicious Catalan salad made from raw salt cod. As the word 'esqueixar' meaning 'to tear' suggests, the salt cod is literally shredded by hand. In Catalunya, market stalls specialising in salt cod sell esqueixada strips to make this dish. The simplicity of this salad does rely on good ingredients: sweet tomatoes and peppers in season, mild onion, fruity olive oil and good vinegar as well as a little time for all the flavours to infuse.

Serves 4

> 300g thick fillet of salt cod (dried weight), washed and soaked in the fridge for 48 hours, changing the water 4 times (see page 83)
> 1 green pepper, quartered, seeded and thinly sliced
> 1 red pepper, quartered, seeded and thinly sliced
> 15 cherry tomatoes (approx. 225g), halved
> 1 large bunch fresh flat-leaf parsley, roughly chopped
> ½ small red onion, sliced wafer-thin
> a handful of small black olives, like niçoises

DRESSING
> 1 garlic clove, crushed to a paste with salt
> 1½ tablespoons good-quality red wine vinegar, or half red wine and half sherry vinegar
> 4 tablespoons extra virgin olive oil
> sea salt and black pepper

Drain the salt cod and remove any skin or bones. Shred the cod between your fingers into soft, fibrous flakes. Transfer to a mixing bowl, and add the peppers, tomatoes, half the parsley and the onion.

For the dressing, whisk the garlic, vinegar and olive oil together, then season with salt and pepper. Pour over the salt cod, and gently toss together. Refrigerate for about an hour. Serve with the remaining parsley and the olives sprinkled on top.

Croquetas de bacalao
SALT COD CROQUETAS

These delectable croquetas are guaranteed to convert those not sure of the merits of salt cod (see page 83). We eat these with alioli and/or sweet tomato sauce. They are also good, eaten cold, on a picnic.

Serves 4

      225g salt cod, soaked for 24 hours in cold water in the fridge

      600ml milk

      2 bay leaves, preferably fresh

      ½ medium onion

      350g potatoes, peeled and quartered

      1 dessertspoon finely grated onion

      1 large bunch fresh flat-leaf parsley, roughly chopped

      1 heaped teaspoon plain flour

      750ml sunflower oil for deep-frying

      1 lemon, quartered

      sea salt and black pepper

While the salt cod is soaking, change the water two or three times. Drain the salt cod and place in a saucepan with the milk, bay leaves and onion half, and bring to the boil. Turn down the heat and simmer very gently for 4 minutes until the fish flakes easily (salt cod will stay more juicy and tender if cooked gently). With a slotted spoon, remove the salt cod and put into a bowl.

Carefully put the potatoes into the same saucepan of simmering milk and cook for 20 minutes or until soft. While the potatoes are cooking, go through the salt cod, discarding any skin and bones. Now mash or shred the cod either between your fingers or with a potato masher. At this point the cod should have no large or hard bits, but just be soft fibre. All of this is best done when the cod is warm, if not hot, as it will become stubborn and gluey when cold. When the potatoes are cooked, drain them, discarding the milk, onion and bay. Put the potatoes through a sieve or mash them well. Now mix the potato with the cod, grated onion, parsley, and the teaspoon of flour. Make sure all the ingredients are thoroughly mixed and check for seasoning.

This is the fun part, shaping croquetas! You will need two dessert-spoons to help provide the basic shape and a board or plate sprinkled with a little more flour to place them on. Scoop some mixture on to your spoon, and with the help of the other spoon make a rough oval egg shape (quenelle). Place it on your floured board. Make twelve to sixteen of these. At this point they are ready to fry, but will keep well for up to 24 hours when covered in the fridge.

When you are ready to eat, put the oil in a large saucepan and place over a medium heat for 4 minutes. Test the temperature by adding a small piece of the cod mixture. It should turn golden brown over the course of a minute, not instantaneously. Adjust the temperature accordingly. Cook the croquetas in two batches, lowering them into the oil with a slotted spoon, until they are amber in colour. When they are ready, lift out with your slotted spoon and place on some kitchen paper. Serve immediately either with Alioli and/or Sweet Tomato Sauce (see pages 248 and 257), a little salad and wedges of lemon.

Almejas con manzanilla
CLAMS WITH MANZANILLA

The Spanish love their 'almejas', clams, in rice dishes, stews or simply steamed open with sherry or white wine. In this recipe we use manzanilla sherry from Sanlúcar de Barrameda. It is a dry sherry with a slightly salty tang, perfect with fish and shellfish. We often serve a glass of chilled manzanilla to drink alongside the clams as the Spanish do.

Serves 4

> 1 kg small clams, such as venus or palourdes
> 4 tablespoons olive oil
> 2 garlic cloves, finely chopped
> 150ml manzanilla sherry (see Sherry Suppliers)
> 1 large bunch fresh flat-leaf parsley, roughly chopped
> 1 lemon, quartered
> sea salt and black pepper

Wash the clams under cold water and rinse thoroughly, discarding any that are open or broken.

In a large saucepan, heat the oil over a medium heat. Add the garlic and fry for a few seconds until it just begins to colour. Add the clams and toss around with the garlic and oil. Pour in the manzanilla and add half the parsley, shaking the pan as you go. Simmer for about a minute to burn off the alcohol in the sherry. When the clams are fully opened (throw away any that are still closed), taste for seasoning. The clams may not need any salt. Sprinkle on the rest of the parsley and serve with lemon and lots of bread or toast.

Warka

'Warka' is the crisp, paper-thin pastry from North Africa that is used to make the famous Tunisian 'briks' (stuffed parcels) or the classic Moroccan 'bisteeya' (sweet, spiced pigeon pie). Warka is for the obsessed and the mad, yet we have taken much pride (and patience) in making it at Moro from the beginning. If you do manage to persevere and succeed, you deserve to have a feeling of genuine achievement. It is a case of 'once you get the hang of it it's easy', but nevertheless very few people outside North Africa make it. We were lucky enough to see it being made in the kitchens of the La Mamounia hotel in Marrakech but, even so, it took a steely determination to succeed.

A FEW TIPS ON MAKING WARKA

- Good flour is important. When we tried to make it with a normal commercial brand of bread flour it didn't have the necessary glutinous elasticity. At Moro we use Shipton Mill organic strong white bread flour.
- The warka dough must sit in the fridge for 45 minutes for the gluten in the flour to develop.
- Wear an apron and old shoes as novices often strew the wet dough over the kitchen and themselves.
- The pan that the sheets of warka are made on is as important as the dough itself. In Morocco they use what looks like an upside-down tray or paella pan made of copper. In this country you will have to be resourceful. A non-stick frying pan that just fits snugly on top of a saucepan is ideal. At home we put a non-stick chapati pan on top of the saucepan and tape both handles together to stop them moving about. If the surface is not non-stick then it must first be cleaned very well and lightly oiled.

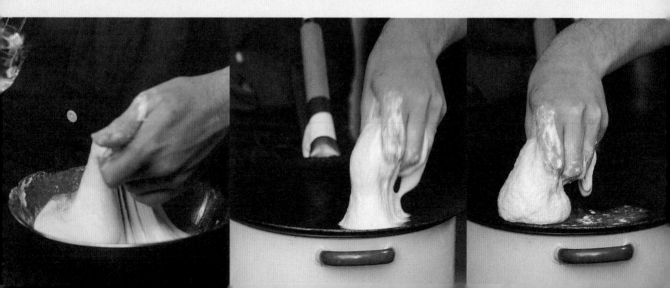

300g strong white bread flour
3 teaspoons sunflower or olive oil
3 teaspoons wine or malt vinegar
300ml tepid water, plus 2 tablespoons

Sift the flour into a large bowl. Mix the oil, vinegar and the 300ml water together in a jug. Slowly start beating the liquid into the flour (a third at a time), using your fingers. Try to beat out the lumps as they appear. Once all the water in the jug is incorporated, beat well with your fingertips for 3 minutes (as if whisking egg whites). Relax in the fridge, covered, for about 45 minutes.

While the warka dough is resting, get your warka pan ready. Fill your saucepan with water to just over half-full and bring to the boil. Reduce to a gentle simmer, and cover with the warka pan. Never let the water run dry.

Remove the dough from the fridge and beat in the additional 2 tablespoons water. The dough should look glossy and smooth. Wash and dry your hands, set a large plate beside you with four pieces of greaseproof paper on top. Briefly beat the warka one more time (this will momentarily strengthen the gluten and make it easier to handle). Pull off a piece of dough the size of a golf ball in your hand, and take a little time to get the feel of controlling it in the palm of your hand. Dab the dough on to the hot warka pan and keep dabbing until you have formed a complete circle with no gaps, of about 25cm in diameter. With the other hand, peel off the pastry and place on the plate in between the paper. There is enough dough for the first two or three sheets to be testers. Continue until you have eight proper sheets. Every now and then give your arm a rest before beating the warka dough and picking up a fresh piece. You can make warka a few hours in advance, but be sure to wrap the plate in clingfilm, as it can dry out and crack. The very best of luck!

Crab brik

Once you have mastered warka, try making our version of the Tunisian brik which, made with crispy warka, moist crabmeat lightly seasoned with cumin, chilli and herbs, is a real treat. At Moro we cook and pick fresh live crabs and although this is quite a laborious process, if you can get hold of fresh crab, we think it is worth it. However, crabmeat from a fishmonger is a good alternative.

Serves 4

   1 crab, about 1 kg in weight, boiled for about 10 minutes, cooled and
      picked thoroughly, keeping the white meat separate from the
      brown, or 400-500g crabmeat, ¾ white, ¼ brown
   1 medium fresh red chilli, halved, seeded and finely chopped
   1 large bunch fresh coriander, roughly chopped
   1 small bunch each of fresh mint and flat-leaf parsley, roughly
      chopped
   ½ garlic clove, crushed to a paste with salt
   2 dessertspoons lemon juice
   ½ teaspoon freshly ground cumin
   sea salt and black pepper

TO FINISH, COOK AND SERVE
8 Warka sheets (see page 90, or see Suppliers)
750ml sunflower oil for deep-frying
Harissa (see page 254)
1 lemon, quartered

If you do a quick job of picking out the meat, or use two smaller crabs instead, 1.25-1.5kg of crab will be necessary. If you pick the crab quickly, you will not get so much, and if the crabs are smaller, there is a higher proportion of shell to meat than in one large crab. Mix the white meat of the crab with the brown meat and add to the rest of the ingredients. Taste for seasoning.

   Lay two sheets of warka on top of each other and put a quarter of the crab mixture into the centre. Lightly moisten the edges with some water and fold them into the centre in a pleating fashion so the crab mixture is sealed inside. Now turn the brik pleat-side down on to a floured surface. Repeat this three more times with your other remaining six pieces of warka.

Put the oil in a large saucepan (never more than half full) and place over a medium heat. Carefully lower one brik at a time into the oil. Cook for a couple of minutes until a beautiful golden brown. When ready, take out with a slotted spoon and pat dry with kitchen paper before serving. Serve with some harissa, the lemon, and a little salad if you like.

VARIATION: As an alternative to crab, try tuna (tinned or raw) with chopped preserved lemon and coriander, or a salted anchovy, harissa and a raw egg cracked in the centre of the warka, which is then folded over and shallow-fried.

Alcaparrones
CAPERBERRIES

Caperberries ('alcaparrones') are the fruit of the caper bush, Capparis spin-
osa, which grows wild throughout the hot Mediterranean. The caper
('alcaparras'), i.e. the flowering bud of the same plant, is more common, but
it is really in Spain where caperberries are most relished. Usually preserved
in vinegar, caperberries are a good accompaniment to fish, or as part of a
sauce or marinade. And as they are less pungent than their cousin, they
can be enjoyed as a simple tapa on their own or mixed with olives. They
should have a firm crunchy texture and not be too large as the seeds can be
slightly gritty. (See Spanish Suppliers)

Octopus salad with dill, paprika and caperberries

Try to get hold of the double-suckered Mediterranean variety of octopus.
These are larger, tastier and more tender than those with a single row of
suckers. Unfortunately they are hard to come by in this country, but give
your fishmonger plenty of warning and encouragement, and he or she might
be able to find one in the fish market. Having said this, there is nothing
wrong with the more common single-suckered octopus that is caught closer
to home, which is probably fresher. With all octopus the most important
thing is to cook it well and long until tender. There are many theories of how
to tenderise an octopus: freezing it, beating it over the rocks by the sea (for
the larger varieties especially), or 'shocking' it in boiling water, the method
we tend to adopt at Moro. This recipe, originally a Turkish mezze, is equally delicious made with squid or cuttlefish which are more readily available,
and simply require being pan-fried briefly before mixing with the marinade.

Serves 4

> 1 small octopus, about 1 kg in weight, or 4 medium squid or
>   cuttlefish
> ½ garlic clove, crushed to a paste with salt
> juice of ½ lemon
> 1½ tablespoons red wine vinegar
> 1 teaspoon sweet smoked Spanish paprika (see page 111)
> 4 tablespoons olive oil
> 1 large bunch fresh dill, roughly chopped
> 200g rocket leaves, dressed with lemon and olive oil
> ½ small red onion, finely sliced in rings
> 20 caperberries
> sea salt and black pepper

Clean the octopus by emptying out the body cavity and rubbing its entirety vigorously under a running water tap – as if you were hand-washing a piece of clothing. Make sure you wash all the sand out of the tentacle suckers. Cut out the eyes and mouth. Bring a large pan of salted water to the boil, add the octopus and put the lid on. When the water comes to the boil again, remove the octopus from the pan and hang for a couple of minutes before returning to the pan. Repeat this one or two more times, then on the last time keep it in the water and simmer until tender. How long it takes to become tender depends on the freshness and variety of the octopus, about an hour, sometimes more, sometimes less.

While it is cooking make a marinade of the garlic, lemon juice, vinegar, paprika, olive oil and chopped dill, and season well. After the octopus has been boiling for about 45 minutes, test to see if it is tender. Cut off a thick bit of the tentacle and taste. If it is tender take it out of the pot. If not, boil it for longer. When it is done, chop it up and toss, still warm, in the marinade. Set this aside for the flavours to mingle for an hour or so.

Serve with the rocket salad, onion, caperberries and extra paprika sprinkled liberally on top.

Deep-fried squid with almonds and bulgur

This is a Lebanese version of the classic deep-fried squid, with the added dimension of bulgur for crunch and almonds for a nutty flavour.

Serves 4

    4 medium-sized squid

    175g whole blanched almonds, finely chopped

    75g fine bulgur wheat (see Lebanese and Turkish Suppliers)

    3 eggs

    5 tablespoons plain flour, seasoned with salt and pepper

    750ml sunflower oil for deep-frying

    1 lemon, quartered

    sea salt and black pepper

Clean the squid by first gently pulling the tentacles and wings free from the body. Keep the tentacles intact by cutting just above where the tentacles join, remove the eyes and mouth and discard. Clean out the guts from the body cavity and remove any skin. Slice the body into 1.5cm rings. Store the rings, tentacles and wings in the fridge until ready to use.

Toss the almonds with the bulgur and season with salt and pepper. Lightly beat the eggs and add a pinch of salt. Dip the squid first into the flour (dusting off any excess), then the egg, and lastly roll it in the almond/bulgur mixture. Lay the dipped squid on a tray and rest in the fridge for half an hour.

In a large saucepan, heat the oil until hot (never more than half full), then fry the squid for about 30 seconds until tender. Season with more salt if necessary and serve immediately with the lemon on the side.

Sardinas a la parilla

GRILLED SARDINES

Grilled sardines are one of the great fish tastes. Whenever we say 'grilled', we ideally mean over charcoal, but this dish will still taste fantastic if cooked under a domestic grill. In the south of Spain, it is common to see sardines staked on a stick, 'al espetón', and grilled over a wood fire. We have recently taken up the habit of sprinkling salt on the fish half an hour before grilling. This slightly firms up the flesh of the fish and imparts a pleasant saltiness. The mixture of chopped olives, parsley, garlic and orange zest cuts through and complements the natural oiliness of the fish.

Serves 4

  8 large or 12 small fresh sardines, scaled and gutted

  3 good pinches sea salt

  1 large bunch fresh flat-leaf parsley, roughly chopped

  2 garlic cloves, finely chopped

  finely grated zest of 2 oranges

  150g cracked green olives, pitted and roughly chopped

  1 lemon, quartered

Scaling sardines is easy: just place each fish under running water and rub as you would a bar of soap. The scales will fall away and any left behind will be easily visible. To gut the fish, make a slit up the length of the belly with a sharp knife or scissors. Wash out the interior of the belly under running water and cut off the fins with scissors. (A fishmonger could easily do all this in a couple of minutes.) Pat the sardines dry with kitchen paper. In a large bowl toss the sardines with the sea salt, cover and chill for about half an hour. Combine the parsley, garlic, orange zest and olives and also chill.

If grilling over charcoal, light a good 30 minutes before you wish to cook. If using a domestic grill turn it to a high heat 5 minutes before you are ready. Grill the sardines for 2–3 minutes on each side until slightly charred but still juicy inside. Sprinkle with the parsley mixture and serve with lemon.

VARIATION: Try parsley, garlic, lemon zest and lightly toasted pinenuts for a change. Or wrap the fish in vine leaves before grilling and serve with Tahini Sauce (see page 255).

Sardinas en escabeche
SARDINE ESCABECHE

'Escabeche' is an ancient method for pickling fish or meat in vinegar, herbs and spices. Back in the times before refrigeration it was an effective way of preserving food other than in salt. Nowadays we make escabeche not just for practical reasons but also to savour all the flavours of the marinade. The saffron and almonds in this particular recipe reflect its Moorish/Andalucían origins.

Serves 4

    8 sardines, scaled and gutted (see page 97), heads on or off
    8 tablespoons olive oil
    4 tablespoons plain flour, seasoned with salt and pepper
    1 small red onion, sliced as thinly as possible into rings
    100g whole blanched almonds, lightly toasted and roughly chopped
    sea salt and black pepper

MARINADE
300ml good-quality red wine vinegar
100ml water
5 bay leaves, preferably fresh
6 garlic cloves, peeled
½ teaspoon black peppercorns
2 teaspoons coriander seeds
1 teaspoon fennel seeds
a good pinch of saffron (about 60 threads), infused in 4 tablespoons
    boiling water (see page 172)
½ teaspoon caster sugar

Salt the sardines inside and out and leave for about half an hour. Meanwhile, make the marinade. Bring the vinegar, water, bay leaves, garlic, black peppercorns, coriander and fennel seeds to a gentle simmer for about 5 minutes to infuse all the flavours. Now add the saffron-infused water and sugar and season with salt and pepper. You will need more salt than you might think because of the acidity of the vinegar. Remove and allow to cool.

    Heat half the olive oil in a large frying pan over a medium heat. Gently dry the sardines on some kitchen paper, dust with flour and carefully place in the pan. Fry each sardine until golden brown on each side and just cooked through, then remove and dry on kitchen paper. Layer the sardines in a dish, sprinkling the onion and almonds as you go, and pour on the marinade followed by the remaining olive oil. Cover with clingfilm and leave in the fridge for at least 24–48 hours (they will keep in the fridge for about a week).

Serve with toast, some caperberries and/or olives, roughly chopped flat–leaf parsley and wedges of lemon. In the mountains, especially during the hunting season, it is common to find 'perdiz en escabeche', partridge escabeche. Saffron is also used in this dish as well as an abundance of the wild herbs, such as thyme and rosemary, that flourish on the mountainsides.

Sardines stuffed with coriander, garlic and cumin

Another memorable sardine experience was in the souk (market) in Safi in Morocco where we ate butterflied sardines stuffed with coriander and cumin and fried in a large copper cauldron of bubbling oil.

Serves 4

8 sardines, of roughly equal size, scaled and gutted (see page 97)

3 garlic cloves, crushed to a paste with salt

1½ teaspoons cumin seeds, roughly ground

1 large bunch fresh coriander, roughly chopped

juice of ½ lemon

300ml sunflower oil

4-5 tablespoons fine semolina flour or plain flour, seasoned with salt and black pepper

To butterfly a gutted sardine, follow the instructions and photographs on pages 196 and 197. Pat the sardines dry with kitchen paper.

For the stuffing, mix the garlic, cumin and coriander and finish off with the lemon juice. Place four of the sardines skin-side down on a tray or large plate. Spread the stuffing evenly over the flesh. Place another sardine (of a similar size) on top, skin-side up, to form a sandwich.

Heat the oil in a large frying pan over a medium heat (never more than half full). Dust each sardine sandwich in flour, shaking off any excess. When the oil is hot, gently place the fish into the pan. Fry for a minute on each side and transfer to some kitchen paper. Alternatively, you can bake the sardines in a hot oven at 220°C/425°F/Gas 7 for about 7-10 minutes. Serve immediately with a green salad or tomato salad if they are in season, lemon and some Harissa (see page 254) if you like a bit of heat.

Revuelto de huevas
SCRAMBLED EGG WITH CURED ROE

The Spanish word for eggs is 'huevos', but when it refers to the eggs of a fish, i.e. the roe, it becomes feminine, 'huevas'. Roe, or 'bottarga' as it is sometimes known, is very popular in Spain, mainly eaten as a tapa, either in thin slices of salted and dried roe, like the highly prized 'huevas de maruca' (ling), or 'huevas de lisa' (grey mullet) or the slightly less delicate 'huevas de atún' (tuna). Roe is also eaten fresh with 'patatas aliñadas' (potato salad with onion, parsley, egg and green pepper dressed with vinegar and olive oil), and we have seen 'huevos de choco' on offer – egg-like forms inside cuttlefish that resemble small white UFOs. At Moro, we serve cured fish roe with 'revuelto' – scrambled egg – and a piece of toast drizzled with olive oil.

Serves 4

>   10 organic or good-quality free-range eggs
>   4 tablespoons milk or cream
>   25g butter
>   100g grated cured fish roe or bottarga (see Suppliers)
>   ½ small bunch fresh flat-leaf parsley, roughly chopped
>   sea salt and black pepper

Lightly whisk the eggs with the milk or cream and season with a little salt and pepper. Melt the butter in a saucepan over a low to medium heat, add the egg and stir slowly with a wooden spoon. The gentle heat will gradually cook the eggs. Remove from the heat when the eggs are the consistency that you like (we prefer them runny and creamy). Divide between four warm plates and quickly sprinkle the roe and parsley over each plate so the egg is more or less covered. Serve with toast.

Mojama

'Mojama' is cured, wind-dried tuna, which is mainly produced in southern Spain in the province of Cádiz along La Costa de la Luz, the Coast of Light. This latter is sometimes (aptly) known as 'El Mar del Atún', the sea of tuna. Interestingly, the word 'mojama' may come from the Arabic 'musama' meaning 'to dry', but it was the Phoenicians who first fished tuna from these waters and learnt to perfect the technique of making mojama: the tuna meat from the back of the fish is filleted into long strips, soaked in salt, washed thoroughly and then hung to dry in the sea breeze for twenty days. The towns of Huelva, Barbate and Ayamonte have perfect micro-climates for producing mojama.

In Spain mojama is served mainly as a tapa but at Moro it has become a popular starter. Mojama requires no preparation other than slicing it as thinly as possible. It is important to slice mojama at the end of your preparation, as it does tend to dry out. Alternatively slice it beforehand and cover it either in olive oil or with a damp cloth. Mojama keeps well wrapped up in the fridge for two to three months. Following are some of our favourite ways of serving mojama. These recipes also work very well with salted anchovies instead. (See Spanish Suppliers)

Left to right: Mojama with piquillo peppers and caperberries; with tomatoes, chopped egg and olives; with spinach, oregano and lemon; with broad beans and mint.

Mojama with spinach, oregano and lemon

This is a light starter. Oregano and marjoram complement spinach very well.

Serves 4

    3 tablespoons olive oil

    1 small garlic clove, thinly sliced

    1 tablespoon chopped fresh oregano or marjoram leaves

    500g spinach, washed (make sure the leaves are not too wet as this can make the cooked spinach a bit watery)

    a squeeze of lemon

    100g mojama (see opposite), sliced as thinly as possible (about 7 slices per person)

    sea salt and black pepper

In a large saucepan, heat the oil over a medium heat. Add the garlic and oregano or marjoram and fry for a few seconds before adding the spinach and a pinch of salt and pepper. Give the spinach a quick stir before putting the lid on, and cook for about a minute. When the spinach is tender, add the lemon juice, stir and check for seasoning. If the spinach is a little watery, drain in a colander. Serve with the mojama on top.

Mojama with piquillo peppers and caperberries

If you cannot source piquillo peppers, you can use fresh red bell peppers and grill them whole until the skins are black and charred all over and the flesh is soft. Allow to cool, peel and seed, then flavour as in the recipe on page 27.

Serves 4

> 200g salad leaves (rocket, gem lettuce or watercress or a mixture)
> 225g Marinated Piquillo Peppers (see page 27)
> Sherry Vinegar Dressing (see page 258)
> 100g mojama (see page 102), sliced as thinly as possible
>   (about 7 slices per person)
> 20 caperberries (see page 94), or a handful of capers
> ½ small bunch fresh flat-leaf parsley, roughly chopped
> 1 lemon, quartered
> sea salt and black pepper

About 5 minutes before you are ready to serve, dress the salad leaves and arrange on four plates, followed by the piquillo peppers, mojama and finally the caperberries and the chopped parsley. Serve with the lemon on the side.

VARIATIONS: We sometimes add a few warmed beans, such as black beans or butter-beans (see page 113 for cooking pulses), that have been dressed in olive oil and sherry vinegar or lemon juice. This is particularly tempting when the weather is less summery, for the beans add a creamy, richer texture to the dish. To assemble, spoon the warm beans with a little bit of their juice on the salad and add the peppers, mojama and caperberries as before. Also, in the spring, young and tender broad beans cooked with mint are delicious with mojama (although a more traditional combination in Spain would be jamón). Follow the recipe on page 114 for how to cook broad beans, then substitute the morcilla for 100g sliced mojama (laid on top at the end) and the chicken stock for water.

Mojama with tomatoes, peppers, chopped egg and olives

This is a good starter for lazy summer lunches outside.

Serves 4

15 cherry tomatoes (about 225g), halved and seeded over a bowl to
retain the juice

2 green bell peppers, halved, seeded and roughly chopped

½ small red onion, thinly sliced

1 large bunch fresh flat-leaf parsley, roughly chopped

2 hard-boiled eggs, roughly chopped

100g mojama (see page 102), sliced as thinly as possible
(about 7 slices per person)

20 small olives, niçoises or arbequina (see Suppliers)

1 lemon, quartered

DRESSING

juice from the seeded tomatoes

1 garlic clove, crushed to a paste with salt

1½ tablespoons red wine vinegar

4 tablespoons extra virgin olive oil

sea salt and black pepper

To make the dressing, strain the tomato juice into a bowl and add the garlic and vinegar. Then whisk in the olive oil and season with salt and pepper.

To assemble the salad, place the tomatoes, peppers, onion, and half the parsley in a large mixing bowl. Pour on the dressing, toss well and leave in the fridge for half an hour to infuse the flavours. Just before serving, add the egg and mix again. Lay the mojama and olives over the salad and finish off with the rest of the parsley and lemon on the side.

Prawns in spiced tomato sauce with caraway

This southern Turkish dish is Mediterranean in feel, but the use of caraway is an example of where the flavours of the eastern Mediterranean and eastern Europe cross over. We buy prawns unshelled as they have a better taste and texture.

Serves 4

   3 tablespoons olive oil

   3 garlic cloves, thinly sliced

   1½ teaspoons whole caraway seeds

   2 small dried red chillies, crumbled

   1 green pepper, seeded and finely chopped

   2 x 400g tins plum tomatoes in their juice

   600g prawns in their shells

   ½ teaspoon caster sugar

   1 small bunch fresh flat-leaf parsley, roughly chopped

   sea salt and black pepper

In a medium-sized saucepan, heat the olive oil and fry the garlic until it begins to colour. Add the caraway and chilli and stir for 30 seconds. Now add the green pepper and soften for 10–15 minutes.

To prepare the tomatoes, pour them into a colander with a bowl underneath. (The leftover tomato juice can be used for other cooking: see page 257 for Sweet Tomato Sauce.) Pinch out and discard the hard stalk of each tomato and put the tomatoes without their juice into another bowl. Break them up well, using either your hand or a fork.

When the peppers are ready, add the tomatoes and simmer for 20 minutes, stirring every now and then. Meanwhile, peel the prawns. Add the prawns to the sauce 3 minutes before the end of cooking, seasoning with the sugar, and some salt and pepper. Serve with the parsley sprinkled on top, some good bread and rocket salad.

MEAT STARTERS

The starters here that are of Spanish origin are typically bold and rich in flavour, and all have a key speciality ingredient which acts as its cultural anchor. The Muslim Mediterranean recipes, however, are lighter and more fragrant, and are characterised by the sparing use of spices as well as the subtle contrasting flavours of yoghurt, blossom waters and fruit.

Pinchitos morunos
MOORISH SKEWERS

'Pinchitos morunos' is an extremely popular tapa in Andalucía. As the name suggests, skewers of meat (originally lamb, but nowadays mostly pork) are marinated in a mixture of Moorish spices and grilled over charcoal. You will need four wooden or metal skewers about 25cm long, or eight of 15cm long.

Serves 4

> 1 pork fillet of 500g, trimmed of fat and sinew
> sea salt and black pepper
>
> **MARINADE**
> ½ heaped teaspoon each of coriander seeds, cumin seeds and fennel
>   seeds, all roughly ground
> 1 teaspoon sweet smoked Spanish paprika (see page 111)
> 2 garlic cloves, crushed to a paste with salt
> a good pinch of saffron (about 60 strands), infused in 2 tablespoons
>   boiling water
> ½ small bunch fresh oregano, roughly chopped, or 1 teaspoon dried
>   oregano
> 1 bay leaf, preferably fresh, crumbled or chopped very finely
> 1 dessertspoon red wine vinegar
> 1 dessertspoon olive oil

Cut the pork fillet in half lengthways and then into 3cm cubes. Flatten these cubes slightly. Place the pork in a large mixing bowl and add the marinade dry spices, garlic, saffron-infused water, oregano, bay and vinegar and mix thoroughly. Then add the olive oil, toss again and leave in the fridge for 2 hours so the flavours of the marinade get into the meat.

Grilling pork over charcoal produces the best flavour, so a good half-hour before cooking, light the barbecue. If cooking inside, turn the grill on to a high setting or use a smoking hot griddle pan. Thread the pork on to the skewers. Grill over a high heat for about 2 minutes each side or until slightly charred on the outside but still juicy inside. Season with salt and pepper. At Moro, we serve pinchitos morunos with a tomato and parsley salad with Sherry Vinegar Dressing (see page 258) and a few pickled chillies.

Manteca colorada
PORK RILLETTES

The Spanish have a delicious recipe for pork rillettes that they make their own by adding paprika and fino sherry. Like the French rillettes, the pâté is sealed by a layer of rendered pork fat and adding paprika colours the fat red giving the dish its name: 'manteca colorada' (coloured lard). Manteca colorada is popular in southern Spain for breakfast; at Moro we serve it as a starter with toast and pickles.

Serves 6-8

    1 kg organic or free-range boneless pork belly, trimmed of rind
    225g pork back fat
    6 garlic cloves, roughly chopped
    1 heaped teaspoon fennel seeds, lightly crushed
    3 bay leaves, preferably fresh, halved
    150ml fino sherry
    ½ teaspoon whole black peppercorns, lightly crushed
    4 teaspoons sweet smoked Spanish paprika (see opposite)
    sea salt and black pepper

Preheat the oven to low, 140°C/275°F/Gas 1.

With a sharp knife, cut the pork belly and the pork fat roughly into 5 x 3cm pieces. Place in a large mixing bowl and add the garlic, fennel seeds, bay leaves, sherry, black pepper, a good pinch of salt and the paprika. Stir well with your hands and transfer to a 2 litre enamel or earthenware terrine, cover tightly with foil so no steam can escape. Place in the middle of the oven for a good 4 hours, until the meat is completely soft and can be shredded easily.

Strain the meat in a sieve and press with the back of a spoon. Put the liquid (fat and juice) aside to cool down, then place it in the fridge (so the fat will rise to the top and solidify). Meanwhile, spread the meat out on a tray until just cool enough to handle, and shred between your fingers, throwing away any bits of fat that have not melted away. This is best done when the pork is warm, if not hot, as it will become more stubborn to shred when cold.

When the pink fat on top of the juice has more or less solidified, spoon off and set aside for later. Add the juice and 2 tablespoons fat to the shredded meat, mix well and season with salt and pepper. The manteca is now ready to put back into a terrine. Line the terrine with clingfilm so you can turn it out later. Pack the meat down gently with the back of a spoon and seal with a layer of the fat about 5mm thick, depending on how much fat was made from the pork. Place in the fridge. The rillettes will keep, sealed, for about one to two weeks. Serve with lots of toast and pickles – we like a mixture of cornichons (small gherkins), olives and pickled chillies.

Paprika

There are two main areas in Spain where 'pimentón', paprika, is produced – Extramadura and Murcia. We use a brand of Spanish paprika called 'La Chinata' which has a smoky aroma and flavour. It can come sweet ('dulce') or hot ('picante'). Before being ground the peppers are dried over oak fires to impart a distinctive smoky quality. Not all paprikas are smoked. (See Spanish Suppliers and supermarkets)

Spanish charcutería

As a reaction against the Arab occupation of Spain, the eating of pork was widely encouraged, and with great effect, for it soon became the nation's most popular meat. 'Charcutería' (cured pork) also became firmly established in the Spanish diet and, traditionally, each household would fatten a pig throughout the year until the 'matanza'. This was an event when family and friends gathered to slaughter the animal and turn it into a myriad of sausages and hams to last the whole year. Never a scrap was wasted. Chorizo, morcilla, salchichón (salami), panceta (belly) and caña de lomo (loin) are some of the better-known products that make up the much-adored Spanish charcutería or 'los embutidos', and all vary greatly in quality according to breed of pig, diet and cure.

Chorizo

Of all the Spanish sausages, chorizo is probably the best known. Its distinct deep-red colour and strong flavour come from one of its main ingredients, paprika. There are many types of chorizo, all different in size, texture, spices and cure (smoked or unsmoked, fresh, semi-cured or cured), and each one varies according to region and tradition. Up in the Sierra Morena above Seville, we had the pleasure of observing one lady's secrets: elbow deep in chorizo meat, she added lots of garlic, anise, sweet and hot paprika, cloves and salt, and then lit a fire in the room where her freshly stuffed sausages were hanging to give them a wonderful smoky aroma. (See Spanish Suppliers)

Chorizo con ensalada de judiones y tomates

HOT CHORIZO WITH BUTTER-BEAN AND TOMATO SALAD

This recipe uses a semi-cured chorizo that requires a little cooking and is eaten hot. We also use an exceptional variety of butter-bean called 'judión', which is plump and luxuriously creamy. This starter makes a light summery lunch when sweet tomatoes are in season.

Serves 4

100-150g judión beans or best-quality butter-beans (see Spanish Suppliers) or cannellini, soaked overnight with a pinch of bicarbonate of soda

20 sweet cherry tomatoes, cut in half

$\frac{1}{2}$ red onion, thinly sliced

1 medium bunch fresh flat-leaf parsley, roughly chopped

Sherry Vinegar Dressing (see page 258)

a drizzle of olive oil

250g mild or spicy cooking chorizo, cut in little pieces

sea salt and black pepper

Rinse the beans, then cover with 2 litres cold water in a large pan. Bring to the boil, reduce the heat to a simmer, and skim off any scum. Cook for 1-2 hours until tender. Pour off the cooking liquid until level with the beans, season and set aside.

To assemble the salad, drain the butter-beans (warm or at room temperature), and put in a bowl with the tomatoes, red onion and parsley. Pour on the dressing and mix well. Let the salad sit for at least 5 minutes to let the flavours mingle. Meanwhile set a frying pan over a medium to high heat. Pour a drizzle of olive oil in to the pan and add the chorizo. As the chorizo is sizzling away, spread the salad on a plate. The chorizo will take only about a minute to cook, really just until crisp on both sides. Spoon the cooked chorizo on top of the salad and serve immediately.

Morcilla

'Morcilla', blood sausage, is common throughout Spain and, like chorizo, has numerous regional variations. Some are flavoured with onion, others with rice, pork fat, pinenuts, almonds, garlic or mint, and spices such as paprika, clove or cinnamon. We adore a piece of grilled morcilla on bread with a cool cerveza (beer) as a tapa, but equally satisfying is tasting them in a bean stew like the famous 'fabada' from Asturias.

Habas con morcilla
BROAD BEANS WITH MORCILLA

One of our most memorable dishes is broad beans with morcilla. Once in Barcelona we came across an unassuming café with a small queue of people outside. We knew it would be worth the wait, and before long we were sitting down to a plate of habas con morcilla. It was April, the season for young broad beans, for each bean was no larger than a fingernail, and like all young vegetables their sweetness and tenderness were exquisite. They had been simply cooked with garlic, mint, a few fennel seeds, and morcilla. Young broad beans are difficult to come by unless you have the luxury of an allotment or kitchen garden, so although time-consuming, large broad beans should be skinned after being blanched for a few minutes.

Serves 4

> 3 tablespoons olive oil
>
> 200g morcilla, cut into rounds about 1–2cm thick
>
> 2 garlic cloves, thinly sliced
>
> ½ teaspoon fennel seeds
>
> 1.5kg broad beans in pods, podded (about 500g podded weight)
>
> 100ml Chicken Stock (see page 175) or water
>
> ½ small bunch fresh mint, roughly chopped
>
> sea salt and black pepper

In a frying pan, heat the olive oil over a medium heat and add the morcilla. Fry for a minute or so until slightly crisp on both sides, trying not to let the morcilla break up too much. Remove from the pan and set aside. Still over a medium heat, add the garlic and fennel seeds and fry for a minute until the garlic begins to colour. Add the broad beans (young or peeled) and the stock or water and cook until the broad beans are tender, about 3–5 minutes. Return the morcilla to the pan to heat through, then stir in the mint and season with salt and pepper. Serve with toast. Sometimes we make this dish with scrambled eggs for a delicious brunch.

Jamón

For us a plate of sliced jamón (cured ham) is one of life's little pleasures, and in the restaurant we serve only the best: Joselito 'jamón iberico de bellota' Gran Reserva from Salamanca, made from semi-wild black-foot pigs that feed on acorns. This diet, coupled with a long cure of about two years, accounts for the jamón's extraordinary sweet flavour, rich deep-red colour and marbled texture that literally melts in the mouth. This is a unique product and, like any special-ity, it is reflected in the price, but it is worth it (see Spanish Suppliers). Jamón iberico from Jabugo, from the Sierra Morena in south-west Spain, is also worth sourcing. As well as the black foot 'jamón de pata negra' from the Iberico pig, there is one other main type of cured ham which is more common, and more suitable for cooking: the white-foot pig ('pata blanca'), 'jamón serrano', available in most supermarkets. Look for the Teruel hams from Aragon.

Croquetas de jamón
HAM CROQUETAS

These delicious crunchy croquetas are simple to make as they follow a sim-ilar procedure to making a white sauce. What is difficult is finding the jamón (cured ham – see above). In the restaurant we simmer a jamón bone in milk, before picking the meat off the bone and use both milk and meat to make the croquetas. This is impractical at home, so instead we gently poach chopped jamón in milk, which works very well.

Serves 6 (makes about 24 croquetas)

800ml milk

½ large onion, studded with 5 cloves

½ teaspoon black peppercorns

2 bay leaves, preferably fresh

a few parsley stalks (optional)

200g jamón serrano (cured ham), very finely chopped

100g butter

150g plain flour

3 eggs

250g very fine dried breadcrumbs

1 litre sunflower oil for deep-frying

Pour the milk into a saucepan and add the onion, peppercorns, bay leaves and parsley stalks (if using). Bring to the boil, then turn down the heat to a gentle simmer to infuse the flavours for 20 minutes. Strain the milk and return to the saucepan and place over a low to medium heat along with the jamón. Simmer for 2 minutes.

In a separate saucepan melt the butter over a low heat. Stir in the flour and cook briefly for 30 seconds. Remove the pan from the heat and slowly add the milk (with jamón bits) to the butter/flour mixture, stirring all the time. Return to the heat and continue to stir until the mixture has come to the boil and thickened. Remove and taste for seasoning. Scoop the mixture out of the saucepan on to a plate or tray, and leave to cool completely.

When you are ready to shape the croquetas, beat the eggs and spread the breadcrumbs out on a plate. To form the basic shape, you will need two dessertspoons. Scoop up some mixture with one spoon, and with the other make a rough oval egg shape (quenelle, see pages 86–7) before gently tipping into the egg. From the egg, transfer (still by spoon as your fingers will become tacky) to the plate of breadcrumbs. Sprinkle liberally with the breadcrumbs, until the croqueta is covered all over. Gently refine the shape of the croqueta in your hand and place on a wooden board or tray. Do this until all the mixture is used up. Refrigerate for an hour (they will keep for up to 24 hours).

When you are ready to eat, heat the oil in a large saucepan over a medium to high heat and fry the croquetas in batches of five until golden brown in colour. Take out and rest on kitchen paper, keeping warm in a low oven if necessary.

In Spain croquetas are often eaten at room temperature, but we eat them hot with a watercress salad tossed with Sherry Vinegar Dressing (see page 258).

Endibias con vinagre de Jerez y jamón

GRILLED CHICORY WITH SHERRY VINEGAR AND JAMON

This recipe balances the rich, salty jamón with the nutty sherry vinegar and bitter chicory.

Serves 4

2 large white chicory heads

½ small bunch fresh flat-leaf parsley, roughly chopped

150g jamón pata negra or serrano (cured ham), thinly sliced (see page 116)

DRESSING

6 tablespoons sherry vinegar (see page 194)

½ garlic clove

½ teaspoon fresh thyme leaves

3 tablespoons extra virgin olive oil

sea salt and black pepper

To make the dressing, put the sherry vinegar into a small saucepan and place over a low heat until it has reduced to about 2 tablespoons. Watch it carefully, as it takes no time to reduce. Crush the garlic and thyme with a good pinch of salt, preferably in a mortar and pestle, until a smooth paste has formed. Now add the reduced vinegar, some freshly ground black pepper and stir in the olive oil. Set aside.

To prepare the chicory, cut off the very end and remove any old, discoloured leaves. Then, keeping the end intact, slice the chicory in half lengthways and cut each half into thirds. Place the chicory on a hot griddle pan, barbecue or grill over a medium heat, and when one side is slightly charred carefully turn them over and grill the other side (this will not take very long). Dress immediately with the dressing, and add the parsley. To serve, fan the chicory out on the plate, and serve the jamón alongside it.

Cecina

'Cecina' is a very distinguished type of Spanish charcutería. It is a deliciously rich, dry piece of cured beef from León in Castilla that is first salted, smoked over oak and then air-cured for about a year. Although not widely available even in Spain, it can be sourced in Britain (see Spanish Suppliers). However, if you do have trouble, it is similar to the Italian bresaola. At Moro, we cover a plate with small thin slices and serve it with either one of the following vegetable accompaniments, depending on the season.

Cecina con remolacha

CECINA WITH BEETROOT AND ALMOND SAUCE

At Moro, we serve this as a starter when young beetroot come into season at the beginning of June. For a more colourful plate, you can use the golden and stripy varieties of beetroot as well as the normal purple.

Serves 4

    500g beetroot, preferably small, and their leaves if possible
    200g cecina, sliced as thinly as possible (see opposite)
    Sherry Vinegar Dressing (see page 258)
    Almond and Sherry Vinegar Sauce (see page 251)
    sea salt and black pepper

First prepare the beetroot. Separate the leaves by cutting 3cm above the bulb and put aside. Wash the beetroot carefully to remove any dirt. Place in a saucepan of cold salted water and bring to a steady simmer. The time it takes for the beetroot to cook will depend on the size, but anything from half an hour to an hour. They will be ready when you can slip a sharp knife easily into the centre of the beetroot, rather like testing to see if a potato is cooked. When the beetroot are ready, remove from the pan with a slotted spoon and set aside to cool slightly before rubbing off the skins. Cut the beetroot into quarters or sixths depending on the size. Now blanch the leaves. When the water is boiling again add the leaves and simmer for a minute or so until the stalk is tender. Drain and cool with cold running water. Gently squeeze any excess water from the leaves.

To serve, dress the beetroot and leaves with the sherry vinegar dressing and divide between individual plates. Lay the cecina randomly on top, with the almond sauce at the side.

VARIATION

Cecina is also delicious with wilted wild garlic leaves. These can be found in woodland all over Britain in spring, and are also wonderful in tortillas or rice dishes. Braise the leaves in olive oil, just like spinach.

Cecina con alcachofas y amontillado

CECINA WITH ARTICHOKES AND AMONTILLADO

The earthy flavours of smoked cecina and nutty amontillado sherry go beautifully with these slightly caramelised artichokes.

Serves 4

  2 large or 4 small globe artichokes
  juice of ½ lemon
  3 tablespoons olive oil
  2 large garlic cloves, thinly sliced
  150ml dry or medium amontillado sherry (see Sherry Suppliers)
  50ml water
  ½ small bunch fresh flat-leaf parsley, roughly chopped
  200g cecina, sliced as thinly as possible (see page 120)
  sea salt and black pepper

To prepare the artichokes, cut the stalks off 5cm from the base, and with a potato peeler peel the tough exterior of what is left of the stalk. The general rule when preparing artichokes is that what is green is tough and what is yellow is tender. Now carefully pull off enough layers of the tough, green outer leaves until you reach the ones that are mostly yellow and therefore tender. Cut the tips off these and peel the base. Scrape out any furry choke with a teaspoon and cut each prepared artichoke in half lengthways and then each half into sixths or eighths. Place in cold water with the lemon juice to stop them discolouring.

Heat the oil in a frying pan over a medium heat, and when the oil is hot add the drained artichokes. Fry for about 3 minutes or until they begin to colour. Now add the garlic and continue to cook until the garlic begins to colour, stirring all the time. Pour in the sherry and reduce almost totally while stirring. Add the water and a little salt and cover with a piece of damp greaseproof paper then a lid to steam the artichokes for about 3 minutes or until they are tender and the water has almost evaporated. Season with salt and pepper and sprinkle on the parsley. Serve either warm or at room temperature with the cecina and some rocket dressed with sherry vinegar and olive oil. These artichokes are also delicious without the cecina.

Grilled quail

Grilling quail over charcoal imparts a wonderful smoky flavour and is a refreshing alternative to grilled chicken. The Turks love to grill quail; the Mangal restaurant on Arcola Road in Stoke Newington in London is a good place to try them. To grill quail yourself, it is important the coals of the barbecue are white and not too hot, otherwise the flesh will char before it is cooked through. For this reason, quail is sometimes wrapped in vine leaves to protect the delicate meat. Rub the tiniest amount of olive oil on to the birds (too much will make the coals flare up), and place breast side up on the barbecue (you can use a hot griddle pan or domestic grill instead). Cook for 5–8 minutes, depending on the heat, then turn over, seasoning with salt and pepper as you do. Cook for another 5 minutes or until the meat is no longer pink but is still juicy.

Charcoal-grilled quail with pomegranate molasses

This is a Lebanese recipe that one of our chefs, Sylvain, gave us. The quails are marinated in treacly pomegranate molasses and spices, and grilled slowly.

Serves 4

4 quails, cut down the middle of the backbone with scissors and flattened out

MARINADE
3 tablespoons pomegranate molasses (see page 125)
1 teaspoon ground cinnamon
½ medium onion, grated
2 garlic cloves, crushed to a paste with salt
a pinch of ground allspice

TO SERVE

200g watercress salad

Pomegranate Molasses Dressing (see page 260)

1 pomegranate, seeds only (the yellow membrane is very bitter)

Mix all the marinade ingredients together and rub well all over the quail. Leave to marinate for at least 2 hours or in the fridge overnight.

To grill the quail, see page 123. Serve with watercress salad dressed with the dressing, and sprinkle the pomegranate seeds on top.

Grilled quail with rose petals

This recipe combines the delicate flavour of quail with the heady scent of roses and, although it may seem an extraordinary combination, it does work very well. If you cannot source rose-petal jam, a good alternative is 75g membrillo (quince paste, see Spanish Suppliers), thinned down with 3 tablespoons rosewater.

Serves 4

4 quails, cut down the middle of the backbone with scissors and
flattened out

MARINADE

1 garlic clove, crushed to a paste with salt

1 level teaspoon ground cinnamon

1 level teaspoon ground cumin

3 tablespoons rosewater (see page 274)

1 tablespoon lemon juice

black pepper

ROSE-PETAL SAUCE

3 tablespoons rose-petal jam (see Turkish Suppliers)

1 small garlic clove, crushed to a paste with salt

¼ teaspoon ground cinnamon

1 tablespoon olive oil

a squeeze of lemon

sea salt and black pepper

Mix all the ingredients of the marinade together and rub all over the quail. Place in a dish and marinate for at least 2 hours or in the fridge overnight.

To make the sauce, mix the rose-petal jam (or membrillo with rose-water), garlic and cinnamon together in a bowl. Add the olive oil and lemon juice and taste for seasoning.

Grill the quail (see page 123) and serve with watercress dressed with oil and lemon and the sauce on the side. Some Iranian shops sell dried rose petals; we like to scatter a few dried or fresh petals over the quail and some roughly chopped pistachios.

Pomegranate molasses

Pomegranate molasses ('dibs rumman' in Arabic) is a syrup made by boiling down the juice of sour Iranian pomegranates until it thickens and changes in colour from red to rich auburn brown. It has a colour and consistency similar to black treacle and is sweet-sour in flavour. Common in Syria and Lebanon, it is used for flavouring soups and stews, sauces, meat and fish, as well as for dressing salads or vegetables, or diluted as a drink.

Quail baked in flatbread with pistachio sauce

This recipe has its roots in Turkey where baking things in flatbread is a part of everyday life and where they are famed for their sauces made with every type of nut. This is one of Moro's classic recipes.

Serves 4
Flatbread dough (see page 18)

FILLING
4 quail
2 pinches ground green cardamom
2 pinches ground black cumin (see page 72) or cumin
3 tablespoons olive oil
1 small bunch fresh flat-leaf parsley, leaves picked from the stalks
sea salt and black pepper

TO SERVE
Pistachio Sauce (see page 257)
1 lemon, quartered

With a small knife, remove the breasts from the quail, discard the skin and set aside. (Keep the legs to roast for a snack sprinkled with paprika.) Marinate the breasts in the cardamom, cumin and salt and pepper. Over a medium to high heat, pour in enough olive oil to cover the bottom of a frying pan. When the oil begins to smoke, add the quail breasts and sear both sides quickly. Remove to a plate.

To make up each stuffed flatbread, first preheat the oven to 230°C/450°F/Gas 8. Divide the dough in four and roll into balls. On a generously floured surface, gently roll each ball with a rolling pin to approximately 5mm thick, making sure the shape is a rough circle about 15cm in diameter. Place the two quail breasts just off centre, with four or five whole parsley leaves, a drizzle of olive oil and another pinch of salt. Fold the uncovered half of the round over to form a half-moon shape and trim the edges neatly. Seal the inside round edge with a little water. Place on an oiled baking tray and bake in the preheated oven for about 10–15 minutes or until the dough is cooked (but not totally crisp) and begins to colour. Serve with the pistachio sauce on the side, some salad and wedges of lemon.

Seared sirloin salad with barley, grapes and sumac

Sumac is a ground red berry that the Turkish, Lebanese and Syrians use traditionally when lemons are not in season, because its sourness is similar to lemons. In this Lebanese recipe sweet grapes balance the tartness of the sumac. It has become one of our favourite dishes.

Serves 4

      50g pearl barley (dried weight)

      2 sirloin steaks, total weight about 500g, about 2.5cm thick

      a drizzle of olive oil

      2-3 bunches fresh flat-leaf parsley, leaves picked from the stalks

      350g white grapes, preferably Muscat (cut in half and seeded) or
          small Sultana (whole)

      sea salt and black pepper

MARINADE

½ small onion, grated

1 tablespoon red wine vinegar

1 teaspoon sumac (see page 155)

1 teaspoon coriander seeds, freshly ground

a pinch of freshly ground allspice

a pinch of freshly ground black pepper

DRESSING

1 small garlic clove, crushed to a paste with salt

1 tablespoon red wine vinegar

4 tablespoons extra virgin olive oil

2 teaspoons sumac

a pinch of freshly ground allspice

a pinch of freshly ground coriander seeds

Simmer the pearl barley in 1 litre water for about 45 minutes or until tender. Drain and set aside to cool.

Mix all the marinade ingredients together and rub evenly over the steaks. Leave to marinate for a good hour or two.

To make the dressing, blend all the ingredients together and season with salt and pepper.

When the sirloin has marinated sufficiently, set a griddle pan over a high heat until it begins to smoke. (You may also use a barbecue.) Rub the steaks with a little olive oil and place on the griddle. For this salad the sirloin needs to be medium rare to rare so it is sufficient to sear the meat on both sides. If your griddle pan is very hot, the meat will need only about half a minute on each side. Season with salt as the sirloin is turned. Remove from the heat and set aside to rest for a minute or so while you assemble the salad.

In a large mixing bowl, place the cold barley, whole parsley leaves and grapes. Pour on the dressing and mix well. Taste for seasoning. Now with a sharp knife cut the steak into thin slices across the grain about 1cm thick. Toss half of the sliced sirloin in with the salad and lay the rest of the strips on top. Serve immediately.

Hummus with ground lamb and pinenuts

Good hummus we all know and love, but the addition of the slightly chewy ground lamb, sweet with onion and cinnamon, is especially delicious.

Serves 4

- 200g chickpeas, soaked overnight with a pinch of bicarbonate of soda
- 6 tablespoons olive oil
- ½ large Spanish onion, very finely diced
- ⅓ teaspoon ground cinnamon
- juice of 1 lemon
- 2–3 garlic cloves, crushed to a paste with salt
- 3–4 tablespoons tahini paste (see page 186)
- 170g lamb, minced
- 2 tablespoons pinenuts, lightly toasted
- 1 medium bunch fresh flat-leaf parsley, leaves picked from the stalks
- a sprinkling of paprika
- sea salt and black pepper

Rinse the chickpeas under cold water, then place in a large saucepan, fill with 2 litres of cold water and bring to the boil. Reduce the heat to a gentle simmer, skimming off any scum as it builds up, and cook for about 1½-2 hours or until the skins are tender. Remove from heat, pour off excess liquid until level with the chickpeas, and season with salt and pepper. Set aside.

Meanwhile, heat half the olive oil over a low to medium heat and fry the onion, stirring occasionally, until golden and sweet. Remove and add the ground cinnamon.

To make the hummus, drain the chickpeas, keeping aside the cooking liquid, and blend in a food processor with a little cooking liquid to help the chickpeas on their way. When smooth, add the lemon juice, garlic, tahini and the rest of the olive oil. Add salt and pepper, and some more liquid if necessary. Taste for seasoning and spread the hummus on to a plate so it is ready to receive the lamb.

Place a frying pan over a high heat and when it is hot, add the caramelised onion and its oil followed by the lamb. Use the back of a fork to break up the lamb as it sizzles and season with salt and pepper. When the lamb begins to crisp, add the pinenuts and transfer immediately to the hummus. Serve with the parsley leaves and paprika sprinkled on top, pickled chillies and plenty of Flatbread (see page 18) or pitta.

Fried liver with cumin

Liver with cumin is one of those perfect combinations. In the restaurant we generally use calf's liver. This basic recipe can be served in a number of ways: below we give some favourite suggestions.

Serves 4

> 2 generous slices calf's liver, total weight 400–500g
> 5 tablespoons plain flour, or semolina flour for a crunchier texture
> 2 rounded teaspoons cumin seeds, roughly ground
> 25g butter
> 1 tablespoon olive oil
> sea salt and black pepper

To prepare the liver, cut into strips about 5cm long and 2cm wide, removing any sinew as you go. Just before frying, season the flour with the cumin, salt and pepper, and dust the liver. Heat the butter and olive oil in a frying pan over a medium heat. When the butter begins to foam, place the liver in the pan. Fry on one side for about a minute until sealed and slightly brown. Turn over and fry for another minute. The liver should be juicy and ever so slightly pink inside.

SUGGESTIONS

We like to serve this liver with roughly broken Crispbread (see page 146), with a salad of cos or gem lettuce, fresh coriander leaves, very thinly sliced red onion, and thin slivers of garlic and whole cumin seeds that have been lightly fried in olive oil. Serve with Yoghurt and Cumin Sauce (see opposite).

Wilted Herb Salad is another successful combination with liver and cumin. Follow the recipe on page 47, and serve with the same yoghurt sauce opposite. Also delicious is fried liver as above, but add a few drops of pomegranate molasses at the end. Serve with watercress or rocket salad with Pomegranate Molasses Dressing (see page 260) and a few pomegranate seeds sprinkled on top.

Fried liver with chopped salad and yoghurt and cumin sauce

This fresh Turkish salad combines beautifully with calf's liver. Yoghurt spiced with cumin is one of those great Middle Eastern tastes. If you have time, try making your own yoghurt (see page 50).

Serves 4

    1 recipe Fried Liver with Cumin (see opposite)
    sea salt and black pepper

CHOPPED SALAD
12 cherry tomatoes
1/2 cucumber, peeled
1/2 small red onion
1 red pepper, halved and seeded
1 green pepper, halved and seeded
1 small bunch each of fresh coriander and flat-leaf parsley
Lemon Dressing (see page 260)

YOGHURT AND CUMIN SAUCE
200g home-made or Greek yoghurt, thinned with 2 tablespoons milk
1 garlic clove, crushed to a paste with salt
1 1/2 teaspoons cumin seeds, roughly ground

Chop the tomatoes, cucumber, onion, red and green pepper finely and place in a bowl. Add the herbs and lemon dressing. Toss well and check for seasoning.

For the yoghurt and cumin sauce, mix the yoghurt with the garlic and cumin, and season with salt and pepper. When the liver is ready, serve immediately with the yoghurt and cumin sauce. Chopped salad is also delicious on its own with the same yoghurt sauce above and Flatbread (see page 18).

Riñones al jerez
KIDNEYS WITH SHERRY

We tasted our first riñones al jerez in a small tapas bar in Murcia. The kidneys were quickly fried in hot olive oil and garlic, then deglazed with a dry sherry and served with fried potatoes sprinkled with paprika to soak up the delicious juice the kidneys and sherry had made. Use either lamb's or the more delicate calf's kidneys and a dry, nutty oloroso or amontillado sherry.

Serves 4

> 6 lamb's kidneys or 1 calf's kidney
> 4 tablespoons olive oil
> ½ large Spanish onion, finely diced
> 1 garlic clove, thinly sliced
> 125ml dry oloroso/amontillado sherry (see Sherry Suppliers)
> a sprinkling of sweet smoked Spanish paprika (see page 111)
> sea salt and black pepper

If the kidneys are still encased in their hard white fat (suet), simply remove and peel off the thin membrane (this is usually done for you). For lamb's kidneys, slice in half lengthways and with a pair of scissors snip out as much of the white gristle as possible without cutting away any of the actual flesh. Then slice each half into bite-size pieces, either in half or thirds depending on the size of the kidney. For the calf's kidney, once the suet and membrane have been removed, cut the kidney more or less according to its natural divisions. Again cut away any gristle and make sure that all the pieces are more or less the same size so they cook evenly.

Heat the olive oil over a low to medium heat and fry the onion, stirring occasionally until golden. Turn up the heat, add the garlic, and fry for 30 seconds, followed by the kidneys. Once the kidneys are sealed on all sides (don't let the onion or garlic burn), season with salt and pepper, add the sherry, reduce the heat and simmer for a minute to burn off the alcohol. It is important the kidneys are ever so slightly pink, tender and juicy in the middle when served. Taste for seasoning. Serve immediately with a sprinkling of paprika and some fried potatoes (see page 232) or bread or salad.

VEGETABLE
STARTERS

These recipes are a balanced, seasonal selection of classic vegetable dishes from Spain and the Muslim Mediterranean, a legacy of the wealth of produce available throughout the region, for its markets are some of the richest and most visually stimulating in the world. They are a good example of how these two culinary cultures complement each other, linked in history by the spread of Islam throughout the Mediterranean, which also had a profound effect on agriculture. Over the course of time, however, diets changed. Spain's has become more fish and meat orientated, while the Muslim Mediterranean still offers a wide selection of vegetable dishes. At Moro we have drawn from all these influences, and while keeping as much of their authenticity as possible, we have made them our own.

Endibias con Picos de Europa
BRAISED CHICORY WITH PICOS CHEESE

Picos, a semi-cured blue cheese, comes from the Valdeón area close to the Picos de Europa mountains in León in northern Spain. It is matured for about three months in damp mountain caves then wrapped in maple leaves. Made from cows' milk in the spring and a blend of cows' and goats' milk in the summer, it has a smooth, creamy texture, a strong smell and is full of flavour, the perfect accompaniment to the lemony and bitter chicory. If you cannot source Picos, Roquefort is a good alternative. Some people say the two cheeses are linked by one of the pilgrimage routes to Santiago de Compostela.

Serves 4

    4 white chicory heads
    1 lemon, halved
    25g butter
    ½ small bunch fresh flat-leaf parsley, roughly chopped
    sea salt and black pepper

    SAUCE
    150g Picos cheese (see Spanish Suppliers), without rind
    140ml double cream
    a pinch of freshly grated nutmeg

Cut the chicory heads into quarters lengthways. Drop into a large pan of boiling, salted water with a lemon half to stop the chicory from discolouring. Bring back to the boil then simmer, covered, for 2–3 minutes until you can easily insert a knife into the heart. Drain in a colander and cool under running water. Gently squeeze the chicory to get rid of any excess water.

Now make the sauce. Coarsely crumble the cheese into a saucepan. Pour in the cream, add the nutmeg and season with pepper (there is no need to add salt as the cheese is salty enough). Warm over a low heat, stirring once or twice, until the cheese starts to melt. When the sauce begins to bubble, remove from the heat (it should still have a few lumps for texture).

Meanwhile, heat the butter in a large frying pan and as it turns nutty brown, add the chicory and braise until it starts to colour and caramelise on all sides. Season with salt and pepper and a good squeeze of lemon. Arrange the chicory on warm plates and spoon over the sauce (warm again if necessary). Serve immediately with the parsley sprinkled on top.

Garbanzos con espinacas
CHICKPEAS AND SPINACH

Both chickpeas and spinach were introduced to Spain by the Moors and are still very much a part of Spanish cooking today. The Moors adopted the sophisticated irrigation systems of the Persians, which enabled them to grow all types of vegetables, pulses and fruit, otherwise almost impossible in the arid south. This recipe comes from Seville and is usually served as a tapa, although it also goes well with meat or fish.

Serves 4

- 200g chickpeas, soaked overnight with a pinch of bicarbonate of soda, or 2 x 400g tins cooked chickpeas, rinsed
- 6 tablespoons olive oil
- 500g spinach, washed
- 75g white bread, crusts removed, cut into small cubes
- 3 garlic cloves, thinly sliced
- ¾ teaspoon cumin seeds
- 1 small bunch fresh oregano, roughly chopped
- 1 small dried red chilli, crumbled
- 1½ tablespoons good-quality red wine vinegar (like Cabernet Sauvignon, see Spanish Suppliers)
- a good pinch of saffron (60 strands), infused in 4 tablespoons boiling water (see page 172)
- ½ teaspoon sweet smoked Spanish paprika (see page 111)
- sea salt and black pepper

Drain the dried, soaked chickpeas in a colander, rinse under cold water, then place in a large saucepan. Fill with 2 litres cold water and bring to the boil. Reduce the heat to a gentle simmer, skimming off any scum as it builds up, and cook for about 1-2 hours or until soft and tender. Remove from the heat, pour off excess liquid until level with the chickpeas, and season with salt and pepper. Set aside.

Place a large saucepan over a medium heat and add half the olive oil. When the oil is hot, add the spinach with a pinch of salt (in batches if necessary), and stir well. Remove when the leaves are just tender, drain in a colander and set aside.

Heat the remaining olive oil in a frying pan over a medium heat. Fry the bread for about 5 minutes until golden brown all over, then add the garlic, cumin, oregano and chilli, and cook for 1 more minute until the garlic is nutty brown. Transfer to a mortar and pestle or food processor along with the vinegar, and mash to a paste. Return the bread mixture to the pan and add the drained chickpeas and saffron-infused water. Stir until the chickpeas have absorbed the flavours and are hot, then season with salt and pepper. If the consistency is a little thick, add some water. Now add the spinach until it too is hot, check for seasoning and serve sprinkled with paprika on top and with fried bread as the Spanish do (or toast).

Artichokes with pinenut, egg and herb sauce

This herby sauce goes very well with artichokes and is also delicious with asparagus. Either make it beforehand, or prepare it while the artichokes are cooking. The artichokes can also be boiled instead of braised. Simply snap off the stalk, trim the leaves and boil whole.

Serves 4

> 8 small or 4 large globe artichokes
> 2 garlic cloves, crushed to a paste with a large pinch of salt
> juice of ½ lemon
> 5 tablespoons olive oil
> sea salt and black pepper

PINENUT, EGG AND HERB SAUCE
2 hard-boiled eggs, peeled and roughly chopped
½ medium red onion, finely chopped
1 small bunch each of fresh dill, tarragon and flat-leaf parsley,
   roughly chopped
½ small bunch fresh mint, roughly chopped
2 tablespoons pinenuts, lightly toasted
½ clove garlic, crushed to a paste with salt
2 tablespoons red wine vinegar
2 tablespoons extra virgin olive oil

Combine all the ingredients for the sauce together in a bowl, and mix well. Season to taste with salt and pepper.

To prepare the artichokes, follow the instructions on page 122, but leave them whole instead of cutting them up. Rub the crushed garlic, lemon juice, salt and pepper over the artichokes, inside and out. Place a large saucepan over a medium heat and add the olive oil. When the oil is hot stand the artichokes upside down and allow to sizzle for a few minutes until they begin to caramelise. Now add enough water to come roughly a third or 1cm the way up the artichokes. When the water begins to boil, turn down to a gentle simmer, loosely cover with a large piece of greaseproof paper and put on the lid. Cook for about 15–20 minutes (depending on size), until they are tender (simply insert a knife in the heart – if it slides in easily, then the artichoke is ready, rather like testing a potato). Check for seasoning, transfer to a plate, and serve with the sauce on the side and Flatbread (see page 18) if you wish.

Espárragos
ASPARAGUS

We always look forward to the asparagus season, which starts at the end of April and lasts through to June. When we go to Spain in the spring we keep our eyes peeled for wild asparagus that grow among the wild flowers along the roadsides. The Navarra region in northern Spain is famous for asparagus, particularly the white variety. Piquillo peppers, also from the same region, when made into a sauce, ideally complement the asparagus.

Asparagus can be served boiled, or can also be lightly grilled after boiling, then served with one of the sauces below.

Serves 4

> 1 kg firm asparagus, green or white
> ½ lemon (if cooking white asparagus)
> 1 tablespoon caster sugar (if cooking white asparagus)
> 1 tablespoon lemon juice
> 4 tablespoons extra virgin olive oil
> sea salt and black pepper

The ends of large asparagus can be woody. Gently flex the very end until the stem snaps off at its natural break, or peel the ends. Rinse, drain and bunch the spears loosely with string. To cook green asparagus, bring a tall saucepan of salted water to the boil, add the asparagus (tips end up) and put on the lid. Boil for 2-4 minutes until tender, depending on the thickness. Drain carefully.

White asparagus spears need to be blanched for longer, for they can be quite bitter if undercooked and therefore need to be served softer. Peel the white asparagus 2cm below the tip, from top to bottom, and cut off the very end. Rinse, drain and bunch loosely with string. Bring a tall saucepan of salted water to the boil with the half lemon and caster sugar, add the asparagus and put on the lid. Boil for about 10 minutes until soft (depending on the thickness), so you can no longer taste any bitterness. Drain.

Dress immediately with the lemon juice, olive oil, salt and pepper, and serve with one of the following sauces: Piquillo Pepper Sauce (see page 250), Pomegranate Molasses Dressing (see page 260), or Romesco (see page 252).

Mushrooms

The two following recipes are a good example of how different regions stamp their cultural identity on 'the mushroom' by using ingredients local to them. At Moro we use wild mushrooms only in season (from August/September until the first frost). If you have trouble sourcing wild mushrooms, a good substitute is gently fried flat field mushrooms with a small proportion of dried wild mushrooms (roughly six parts field to one part wild). The dried mushrooms we recommend for flavour are porcini (boletus/cep) and morel. Simply cover with boiling water and let them stand for 10 minutes. Meanwhile clean the field mushrooms and slice roughly. Heat about 4–5 tablespoons olive oil and fry 2 chopped garlic cloves until they begin to colour. Immediately add the field mushrooms with a pinch of salt and pepper and fry gently for 15–20 minutes, stirring occasionally. Then stir in the chopped, soaked dried mushrooms and their juice and fry for a further 5 minutes until the liquid has more or less evaporated. Season.

Mushrooms with wheat berries

Wheat berries are hulled whole grains of wheat that have an interesting, slightly chewy texture, usually used in soups, pilavs or puddings. They are available in Lebanese shops. You could use pearl barley instead.

Serves 4

50g wheat berries (dried weight)

½ onion

400g wild mushrooms, such as chanterelles, trompettes de mort, porcini, pieds de mouton, oyster (or the equivalent of dried and field – see above for how to cook)

5 tablespoons olive oil

2 garlic cloves, roughly chopped

1 level teaspoon ground cumin

1 small bunch fresh coriander, roughly chopped

juice of ½ lemon

sea salt and black pepper

Simmer the wheat berries in 1 litre water with the onion for 40-60 minutes or until tender, then drain. Pick over the mushrooms for any bits. If they are particularly dirty, wipe them with a damp cloth. Slice the mushrooms up roughly. Heat the olive oil in a large frying pan over a medium heat and add the garlic. As soon as it starts to colour, add the cumin and mushrooms. Stir for a minute, lower the heat and fry for about 5 minutes until soft. Then add the wheat berries, coriander, lemon juice, salt and pepper to taste. Serve with warm Flatbread (see page 18), a little spiced yoghurt and salad on the side.

Setas al jerez
MUSHROOMS WITH SHERRY

Serve these mushrooms with toast rubbed with garlic and olive oil.

Serves 4

400g wild mushrooms, such as chanterelles, trompettes de mort, porcini, pieds de mouton, oyster (or the equivalent of dried and field – see page 143 for how to cook)

5 tablespoons olive oil

1 small onion, finely chopped

1 garlic clove, finely chopped

150ml fino (or dry, old amontillado) sherry (see Sherry Suppliers)

a pinch of freshly grated nutmeg

1 small bunch fresh flat-leaf parsley, roughly chopped

sea salt and black pepper

Prepare the mushrooms as for the recipe above and slice roughly. Heat the olive oil in a large frying pan, then add the onion. Cook gently for about 10 minutes until golden and sweet, then add the garlic and cook for 1 more minute. Turn up the heat, add the mushrooms and cook for about 5 minutes until soft, stirring every so often. Now add the sherry and nutmeg and cook for 1 more minute, followed by the parsley, salt and pepper.

Revuelto de setas

SCRAMBLED EGG WITH MUSHROOMS

The last time we were in Spain in the late autumn, north of Seville, among forests of cork oak and chestnuts, we caught the end of the mushroom season. In the local town of Aracena we shared a memorable 'revuelto' (scrambled egg), with fresh porcini mushrooms and strips of the famous black-foot jamón (cured ham) from Jabugo which is only a half-hour drive from Aracena. It was rich but very, very delicious – perfect with a glass of the local 'tinto' (red wine). With or without jamón, it is an excellent dish.

Serves 4

500g wild mushrooms, mixed, or one variety such as porcini, chanterelles, pieds de mouton or oyster, (or a mixture of dried wild and field – see page 143 for how to cook)

3 tablespoons olive oil

1 garlic clove, finely chopped

25g butter

6 organic or free-range eggs, cracked into a bowl but not whisked

3 tablespoons milk

40g sliced jamón pata negra or serrano (optional), cut into 2cm strips (see page 116)

1 tablespoon roughly chopped fresh flat-leaf parsley

sea salt and black pepper

First pick over the mushrooms for any bits. If they are particularly dirty, wipe them with a damp cloth. Slice the mushrooms up roughly. Set a large frying pan over a medium heat and add the olive oil. When the oil is hot, add the garlic and fry for a minute until it begins to colour. Immediately add the mushrooms and stir well. Fry for 3–5 minutes until the mushrooms are soft, adding the jamón a minute before they are ready, then season with salt and pepper and transfer to a bowl. In the same frying pan, melt the butter. Now add the eggs and milk and stir with a fork or wooden spoon so the eggs break up. When they begin to set, return the mushrooms to the pan, along with the parsley, and continue cooking until the white of the egg is more or less cooked. Serve immediately with toast.

Feta salad with spinach, crispbread, sumac and pinenuts

This is a colourful, crunchy salad that has a fresh, interesting tartness to it from the combination of the feta and sumac.

Serves 4

      500g young, tender spinach, washed and spun dry
      200g good-quality feta cheese, crumbled
      1 dessertspoon fresh oregano or marjoram leaves
      75g pinenuts, very lightly toasted

CRISPBREAD

      25g butter
      2 pitta breads

DRESSING

      ½ garlic clove, crushed to a paste with salt
      1 tablespoon good-quality red wine vinegar (Cabernet Sauvignon, see Spanish Suppliers)
      2 teaspoons sumac (see page 155)
      4 tablespoons extra virgin olive oil
      sea salt and black pepper

To make the crispbread, preheat the oven to 180°C/350°C/Gas 4. Melt the butter, and as it is melting, carefully split the pitta in half lengthways and brush the butter on both sides. Place the pitta halves on a rack in the middle of the oven. Bake for about 10–15 minutes or until golden brown. Remove and cool.

For the dressing, whisk all the ingredients together and taste for seasoning.

To assemble the salad, put the spinach, roughly broken crispbread, half the feta, the oregano or marjoram and pinenuts in a large mixing bowl. Pour on most of the dressing and give everything a good toss. Serve with the remaining feta and dressing on top and warm Flatbread (see page 18).

Pinenuts

An early childhood memory was of hours spent cracking open the shells of pine kernels to extract the delicate, creamy nut from within. Pinenuts, especially the Mediterranean variety, have a resinous flavour and ever so slightly waxy, chalky texture. They are highly prized and superior to the Asian variety, so more expensive. They are used in all fields of cooking throughout the Mediterranean – in sauces, salads, rice dishes, sweets and omelettes such as the one on page 153.

Feta wrapped in vine leaves

This recipe is a variation on the classic grilled haloumi cheese. The vine leaves protect the feta from the heat of the grill and give it an interesting flavour. You can find them mainly in Greek, Turkish and Lebanese shops. We serve this with a salad of oranges (blood oranges when they are in season), parsley and olives. You will need four small wooden skewers.

Serves 4

16–32 vine leaves (1 small jar) in brine

400g feta cheese, in pieces about 4–5cm square and 2cm thick (you need 16 in total, 4 per skewer)

1 teaspoon dried oregano

ORANGE SALAD

4 oranges, rind and pith removed and cut into rounds 1cm thick

a drizzle of extra virgin olive oil

1 large bunch fresh flat-leaf parsley, leaves picked from the stalks

20 oily black olives

sea salt and black pepper

Soak the vine leaves for about an hour in two changes of cold water to take away the strong tang of the brine, then drain and pat dry. Pinch out any stalks. Sprinkle the feta with the oregano. To wrap the feta, flatten out one or two vine leaves, depending on the size (if two, make sure they overlap), and place the piece of feta at one end. Wrap the leaf around the feta until the cheese is entirely covered. Carefully thread on to the skewers.

For the salad, arrange the orange rounds on a serving plate, drizzle olive oil on top and add a little salt and pepper, the parsley leaves and olives.

If you are using a barbecue to cook the feta, make sure the heat is very gentle and grill on both sides for a couple of minutes each. With a domestic grill, however, the heat is less direct, so it can be higher and the cheese may require a little more time. The feta is ready when it is soft (but not too soft) to touch. It is important the vine leaves do not char too much, as they are delicious to eat, especially when they go slightly crispy. Lay the skewer on the salad and eat immediately with bread.

Broad bean and fava bean purée

The classic, earthy Egyptian fava bean purée (dried broad beans) inspired us to make a purée from fresh broad beans and to serve the two together as a starter with Flatbread (see page 18). This also makes a good mezze.

Serves 4

FRESH BROAD BEAN PUREE

1 kg fresh broad beans, podded, or 300g already podded

1 garlic clove, crushed to a paste with salt

a squeeze of lemon

2 tablespoons olive oil

1 small bunch fresh mint, roughly chopped

sea salt and black pepper

FAVA BEAN PUREE

125g dried fava beans, soaked overnight then drained

5 tablespoons olive oil

3 garlic cloves, thinly sliced

1½ teaspoons cumin seeds, roughly ground

a squeeze of lemon

1 bunch fresh coriander or dill, roughly chopped

Caramelised Crispy Onions (see page 172)

sea salt and black pepper

Bring a saucepan of unsalted water to the boil and add the fresh broad beans. Cook for about 5 minutes or until soft. Drain, then transfer to a food processor or mouli and purée until smooth. Transfer to a bowl, then add the garlic, lemon juice, olive oil and mint, and season with salt and pepper.

For the fava bean purée, in a large saucepan heat the oil over a medium heat. Add the garlic and cumin and fry until golden brown. Now add the fava beans, stir well and cover with water. Cook for 10 minutes or more over a low heat until the beans are completely soft, adding more water if necessary. Transfer the beans to a bowl and mash to a thick paste. Season with salt and pepper and a squeeze of lemon, then add the chopped herb and another dash of olive oil. Finally stir in most of the caramelised crispy onions, sprinkling the remainder on top.

Poached eggs with yoghurt, sage and chilli flakes

We wish we had a nostalgic tale of the time we tasted this dish on one of our trips to Turkey, but this is actually an adaptation of a recipe we found on the Internet. Although it sounds very simple, the dish is made special by the sweet and crispy sage, caramelised butter and fiery chilli flakes.

Serves 4

    1 small bunch fresh sage, leaves picked from the stalks
    1 garlic clove, crushed to a paste with salt
    350g home-made or Greek yoghurt, thinned with 2 tablespoons milk
    75g butter
    1 dessertspoon vinegar (any)
    4 organic or free-range eggs
    1 teaspoon Turkish chilli flakes (see Turkish Suppliers) or paprika
    sea salt and black pepper

First make the caramelised butter, following the instructions on page 70. Then transfer as much of the clear butter as possible (no bits) to a small saucepan. Heat until hot, add the sage leaves and fry quickly for a few seconds, preferably until crisp. Do not let the sage or butter burn. Remove from the heat, place the sage on kitchen paper, and return the butter to the caramelised bits. Set aside.

Put a large pan of water over a high heat. While you are waiting for the water to boil, mix the garlic with the yoghurt and taste for seasoning. When you are ready to eat and the water is boiling, turn the heat down low, and add the vinegar and a pinch of salt. With a wooden spoon, stir the water rapidly in one direction. Break the eggs, one by one, into the water.

While the eggs are setting, lay out four plates and put a large dollop of garlicky yoghurt in the centre of each. Carefully spread out, making a small well in the middle for the egg. When the eggs are cooked to your liking, drain them of water and lay each one in the middle. Season with salt and pepper. Warm up the butter and spoon over the yoghurt and eggs. Finally place the sage leaves and chilli flakes or paprika on top.

Aubergine and red pepper salad with caramelised butter and yoghurt

This is one of our favourite Turkish dishes, also delicious with grilled lamb. The aubergine has a luxurious and rich texture.

Serves 4

    3 large aubergines

    3 red peppers

    1 garlic clove, crushed to a paste with salt

    a squeeze of lemon

    2 tablespoons olive oil

    200g home-made or Greek yoghurt, thinned with 2 tablespoons milk and seasoned with salt

Caramelised Butter (see page 70)
a few sprigs of fresh coriander
sea salt and black pepper

Pierce the skins of the aubergines and peppers to prevent them from exploding, and grill whole over a hot barbecue, under a grill, or directly on the naked flame of a gas hob until the skin is charred and crispy all over and the flesh is very soft. If none of these options is available, place in a very hot oven at 220°C/425°F/Gas 7 for about 45 minutes until soft. When cool enough to handle, strip off the skins.

Roughly chop the aubergines, then add the garlic, lemon juice and olive oil, and season. Spread this on a plate. Seed the red peppers, chop up roughly, season and strew over the aubergine. Pour the yoghurt over one side of the aubergine and pepper, and spoon the warm caramelised butter on top. Finish with the coriander, and scoop up this delectable salad with some warm Flatbread (see page 18) or pitta.

Courgette omelette with pinenuts, herbs and sumac

Cooking an omelette to perfection can be an art, but with the combination of these ingredients this omelette will never be anything but delicious. When toasting pinenuts, toast them very lightly (until just golden), or their texture may be compromised, and their flavour may become too strong.

Serves 4 (makes 4 omelettes)

    4 medium courgettes, thinly sliced

    7 tablespoons olive oil

    3 garlic cloves, finely chopped

    6 eggs, organic or free-range

    2 tablespoons milk

    100g butter

    2 small bunches fresh flat-leaf parsley, roughly chopped

    1 small bunch each of fresh mint and dill, roughly chopped

    1 tablespoon pinenuts, lightly toasted

    $1\frac{1}{2}$ teaspoons sumac (see page 155)

    sea salt and black pepper

Toss $\frac{3}{4}$ teaspoon fine sea salt with the courgettes and leave to drain in a sieve or colander for half an hour. Then lightly squeeze out the excess salty water. In a large frying pan over medium heat, heat 3 tablespoons of the olive oil, and fry the garlic until it begins to colour. Now add the courgettes and cook until soft, about 5-10 minutes. Season with pepper and set aside, but keep warm.

    Whisk the eggs with the milk and a pinch of salt. For each omelette, in a frying pan about 15-20cm in diameter, heat up 1 tablespoon of the olive oil and 25g of the butter over a medium to high heat. When the butter begins to foam, pour roughly a quarter of the egg mixture into the pan, and swirl the pan to get a thin layer over the bottom. Almost immediately spoon in a line of courgettes, mixed herbs and pinenuts, using a quarter of each. The omelette takes only a few seconds to cook. With tongs or a spatula, roll the omelette into a fat sausage and slide off on to a warm plate. Repeat for the other three omelettes, and serve with sumac sprinkled on top.

Fattoush

This Lebanese bread salad makes a delicious starter or light lunch in summer. Za'tar is a herb that is found growing wild in Lebanon and which tastes similar to thyme and savory. It is very difficult to find fresh za'tar over here but a dried version, with sesame seeds and sometimes sumac, can be found in Lebanese and Turkish shops. This is often mixed with olive oil and served with flatbread.

Serves 4

>   Crispbread (see page 146)
>   ½ large cucumber, peeled, halved, seeded and cut into 1cm dice
>   12 ripe cherry tomatoes, cut into quarters
>   ½ medium cauliflower, broken into tiny florets roughly the same size
>   as the tomato
>   1 spring onion, finely chopped
>   6 radishes, cut into sixths or quarters, depending on size
>   1 celery stick, chopped (optional)
>   1 small bunch each of fresh mint, coriander and flat-leaf parsley,
>   roughly chopped

DRESSING

1 garlic clove, crushed to a paste with salt
juice of ½ lemon
1 teaspoon sumac (see opposite)
1 teaspoon za'tar (see Lebanese and Turkish Suppliers)
5 tablespoons extra virgin olive oil
sea salt and black pepper

For the dressing, combine all the ingredients and taste for seasoning. About 5 minutes before you are ready to serve the salad, combine the crispbread, vegetables and herbs in a large salad bowl, breaking up the bread in your hands as you go. The crispbread should be about the same size as the chopped vegetables. Now add the dressing and toss well until everything is covered. Taste for seasoning.

Sumac

 The sumac tree grows wild throughout the eastern Mediterranean, and it produces a small, red berry that is harvested at the end of the summer, dried in bunches and then ground to a powder that varies in colour from deep red to maroon. This powder is used in Lebanese, Syrian and Turkish cooking especially. It has a sour lemony flavour (traditionally substituted for lemons when they were out of season), and is used among other things to season salads like Fattoush, chicken, yoghurt and kebabs. It is available in Lebanese and Turkish shops (see Suppliers).

Fatayer

Fatayer are stuffed triangles of flatbread from Lebanon and Syria. The traditional fillings are spinach and labneh (yoghurt cheese). This is our version, using pumpkin, feta and pinenuts. The choice of pumpkin is key, for many can be stringy and insipid. At Moro we make these fatayer in the late summer/early autumn when pumpkins and squashes are in season. We use the Hubbard or Crown Prince varieties which are dense and sweet, but Kabouchi or Butternut work well and are more readily available. Indian/Bengali shops often have good-quality pumpkins.

Serves 4

FATAYER DOUGH

220g strong white bread flour, plus a little extra for dusting

$\frac{1}{2}$ teaspoon sea salt

$\frac{1}{2}$ teaspoon dried yeast

100ml tepid water

2 tablespoons olive oil

FILLING

800g pumpkin or squash, peeled, seeded and chopped into 5cm
    square chunks

$\frac{1}{2}$ garlic clove, crushed to a paste with salt

1 tablespoon olive oil

80g feta cheese, crumbled and mixed with $\frac{1}{2}$ small bunch fresh
    oregano, chopped

1 tablespoon pinenuts, lightly toasted

sea salt and black pepper

To make the fatayer dough, place the flour and salt in a large mixing bowl. Dissolve the yeast in the water and then pour the oil into the water. Now pour the water into the flour a bit at a time while mixing. We like to do this by hand, squelching out the lumps as they appear. When all the water is added, transfer to a floured surface and knead well. If the dough is still sticky add a little more flour; if it is still crumbly add a little more water. Continue kneading for about 5 minutes until the dough is no longer tacky, but soft,

elastic and smooth. Set aside to rest on the floured surface covered by a cloth.

Meanwhile, preheat the oven to 230°C/450°F/Gas 8. To start the filling, toss the pumpkin in the garlic and olive oil, and season. Place on a baking tray in the preheated oven for about 25 minutes or until soft. Remove and cool. Purée and taste for seasoning.

To make up the fatayer, divide the dough in four and roll into balls. On a generously floured surface, using a rolling pin, gently roll each ball to approximately 5mm thick, making sure the shape is a rough circle about 17cm in diameter. Put 1 rounded tablespoon of the pumpkin filling in the middle of each circle, shape it into a vague triangle and put a quarter of the feta (with oregano) and pinenuts on top. Moisten the edge of the circle with a little water, then lift the dough into the centre around the triangle of pumpkin. With your fingers, gently squeeze the adjoining edges together until sealed. Trim the edges of the triangle of any excess dough and pinch together again.

Place the four fatayer on an oiled baking tray and bake for about 10–15 minutes in the preheated oven, or until the dough begins to colour, but not totally crisp.

Serve with a rocket salad and Tahini Sauce (see page 255). Or, if served with Braised Chard or spinach (see page 234), or Chickpea Salad (see page 246), it would make a balanced main course.

Getting to know paellas and pilavs over the past few years has been a revelation. We make no pretence that there is much similarity between the two apart from they are both classic rice dishes that are underestimated and underused. We hope that in reading this chapter you will become familiar with their respective secrets and techniques, and be inspired to make them often.

PAELLA

The word for paella is commonly understood, but we sometimes call our rices 'arroz' (plural, 'arroces'), which is a word of Arab origin for rice dishes. We love the look of them, the smell of them and the taste of them, and as long as you take care to soften an onion properly, you will find them easy. Unlike risotto, paella is not served saucy and wet, but each grain of rice should lightly glisten with olive oil yet never seem greasy. Using a chicken or fish stock is beneficial but not always essential, as the main body of flavour in an arroz comes from the 'sofrito' (softened onions, garlic and peppers), and the meat or fish that is cooked with the rice. Taking the time to get the sofrito softened and sweet is important. Also remember that, unlike risotto, arroz should not be stirred, as this can disrupt the way it looks and cooks. A better way to prevent sticking is to gently shake the pan halfway through cooking and to gradually turn down the heat as the liquid vanishes.

On our honeymoon, we went to Valencia with the hope of tasting a paella by which all others would be judged. However, we were unlucky in our quest and ended up judging what we ate very harshly. Back at Moro, the more we made, the more our understanding of and belief in the dish increased, and we are now very proud of the rices we serve.

WHAT TYPE OF RICE?
Valencia and Murcia are wonderful cities and both regions still boast a network of Moorish irrigation systems which make it possible to grow much of Spain's paella rice. At Moro, we use calasparra rice that is grown in Murcia. It is a short-grain rice that has a wonderful ability to absorb liquid and flavour without losing its texture (see Spanish Suppliers).

Arroz negro
BLACK RICE

This rice is far subtler than its appearance would suggest. The squid ink that colours the rice is as much about the luxurious texture it provides as about flavour. It is important to have a good fish stock for this rice, and for your onions and peppers to be cooked and sweet. Once served, you will know if this dish has been a success because you should have black-lipped and black-toothed grins from your diners.

Serves 6 as a starter, 4 as a main course

    6 tablespoons olive oil

    600g squid, cleaned (see page 188) and sliced

    1 large Spanish onion, finely chopped

    2 medium green peppers, halved, seeded and finely chopped

    3 garlic cloves, finely chopped

    250g calasparra (paella) rice (see Spanish Suppliers)

    100ml white wine

    1 litre hot Fish Stock (see page 175)

    10 individual (4–5g) sachets squid or cuttlefish ink (from a
        fishmonger or good delicatessen)

    1 dessertspoon tomato purée

    1 small bunch fresh flat-leaf parsley, roughly chopped

    1 lemon, in wedges

    sea salt and black pepper

Place a 30–40cm paella pan or frying pan over a medium to high heat and add 2 tablespoons of the olive oil. When hot, carefully add the squid to the pan and stir-fry for 30 seconds. Lift the squid out of the pan with a slotted spoon and put to one side. Add the rest of the olive oil to the pan along with your chopped onion and pepper. Stir regularly, still over a medium heat, for 5 minutes to get the initial softening under way. Turn the heat down to low to medium and cook for a further 10 minutes, again stirring regularly. Now add the garlic and cook for 10 more minutes. The peppers, onions and garlic should be sweet, soft and with some colour at this point. Add your rice to the pan and coat with the oil and vegetables. (Up to this point everything can be cooked in advance. The next stage requires about 20 minutes more cooking time.)

Pour in the white wine and let it simmer for half a minute before adding the stock. Snip a small hole in each sachet of ink and squeeze them into the rice (there is no unmessy way of doing this!). Stir in the tomato purée and half the chopped parsley and season perfectly with salt and pepper. From now on do not stir the rice, just simmer gently and shake the pan to prevent it from sticking. When the rice starts rising above the stock, scatter the squid over the rice, and cook for 4 more minutes, still over a low heat (or until there is just a little juice left at the bottom of the paella pan). Cover the pan tightly with foil and let it sit for 3–5 minutes. Serve with the rest of the parsley on top, some salad, Alioli (see page 248) and wedges of lemon.

Paella de pollo con alcachofas y oloroso
RICE WITH CHICKEN, ARTICHOKES AND OLOROSO

This richly flavoured rice dish is the perfect excuse to go out and find a decent bottle of old, and therefore not too sweet, oloroso (see Sherry Suppliers) and reward yourself with a tipple when you return.

Serves 6 as a starter, 4 as a main course

> 6 tablespoons olive oil
> 350g boned and skinned chicken, cut into 2cm cubes
> 2 large Spanish onions, finely chopped
> 3 large globe artichokes
> 6 garlic cloves, finely chopped
> 250g calasparra (paella) rice (see Spanish Suppliers)
> 150ml medium to dry oloroso or old dry amontillado sherry
> 800ml hot Chicken Stock (see page 175)
> 1 small bunch fresh flat-leaf parsley, roughly chopped
> 4 grates of nutmeg
> 1 lemon, in wedges
> sea salt and black pepper

Heat a 30–40cm paella pan or frying pan over a medium to high heat and add 2 tablespoons of the olive oil. When hot, stir-fry the chicken for 2 minutes or until fractionally rare in the middle. With a slotted spoon remove the chicken and put to one side. Add the rest of the olive oil and the onions and soften over a medium heat for 20 minutes, stirring now and then. Meanwhile, prepare the artichokes (see page 122). Cut each artichoke in half and each half into eight wedges. Add the artichoke to the softening onion along with the chopped garlic and cook for another 10 minutes or until the onions and garlic have some colour (caramelisation) and sweetness. Stir in the rice and coat in the oil and vegetables for 1 minute. (Up to this point everything can be cooked in advance. The next stage should be started about 20 minutes before you wish to eat.)

Turn the heat to medium to high, and add the sherry. Cook off some of the alcohol for a minute, then add the stock. Bring to a gentle boil, season well at this point, then add half the chopped parsley and the nutmeg. Simmer for 10 minutes or until there is still enough stock to cover the rice. Spread the chicken evenly over the rice and then push each piece of chicken under the juice. Gently shake the pan to help prevent it sticking and turn the heat down to medium to low. Cook for 5 more minutes or until there is just a little liquid left at the bottom of the rice. Turn off the heat, cover tightly with foil, and let the rice sit for 3–5 minutes before serving. Serve with the rest of the parsley on top, a salad and the lemon.

Dried Spanish peppers

Spain uses a wonderful variety of peppers in cooking. Dried peppers add their own quality to the famous Spanish rices and sauces. At Moro, we use three varieties – the first two are sweet ('dulce'), the last hot ('picante'). To use them, break open and discard the seeds and stalks. Tear into small pieces, cover with boiling water and leave to infuse until soft.

'Ñora' is a small, round red pepper, no larger than a plum, whereas the 'choricero' is bell-shaped. Both the ñora and choricero have a wonderful, sweet, earthy flavour. 'Guindilla' is a spiky pepper, like a large red chilli, which gives heat to a dish. (See Spanish Suppliers)

Sweet and hot paprika can be substituted if you are unable to source the peppers, although the flavour is not quite the same.

Paella de cerdo con chorizo y espinaca

RICE WITH PORK, CHORIZO AND SPINACH

This rice is very Spanish in taste. A complex and comforting dish.

Serves 6 as a starter, 4 as a main course

    7 tablespoons olive oil

    350g pork fillet, halved lengthways, then sliced across roughly into
        7mm strips

    120g mild cooking chorizo, cut into little pieces

    2 large Spanish onions, finely chopped

    1 large green pepper, halved, seeded and finely chopped

    4 garlic cloves, finely chopped

    250g calasparra (paella) rice (see Spanish Suppliers)

    1 teaspoon sweet smoked Spanish paprika (see page 111)

    2 ñoras peppers (to prepare, see page 163)

    900ml hot Chicken Stock (see page 175) or water

    500g spinach, washed and drained

    1 lemon, in wedges

    sea salt and black pepper

In a 30–40cm paella pan or frying pan, heat the olive oil over a high heat, then stir-fry the pork for a few seconds so it is still a little undercooked. Season with salt and pepper. Remove from the pan with a slotted spoon and put to one side. Turn down the heat to a low to medium temperature and fry the chorizo for a minute. Add the onion and green pepper and cook for 20 minutes, stirring occasionally. Add the garlic to the onion and cook for a further 5–10 minutes. At this point the mixture (sofrito) should have caramelised and taste sweet. Stir the rice into the pan to coat in the flavoursome mixture for a minute. (Up to this point everything can be cooked in advance. The next stage requires about 20 minutes more cooking time.)

Now season with salt and a little pepper, for this is the time to season the rice perfectly. Add your paprika and ñoras peppers, drained of their water, followed by the hot stock, and simmer for 15 minutes or until there is just a thin layer of liquid around the rice.

Meanwhile in a large saucepan or wok, briefly wilt the spinach with a little salt, either by braising or steaming, and put to one side with the pork fillet. Evenly scatter the pork over the rice followed by the spinach. With the back of a spoon gently push the pork and spinach partially into the oily liquid that remains at the bottom of the pan. Cover the paella tightly with foil and let it sit for 3–5 minutes. Serve with lemon and a tomato salad.

Paella de rape con azafrán
MONKFISH RICE WITH SAFFRON

Clams or prawns can be added to this rice with great success. Put the prawn shells in the stock for extra flavour.

Serves 6 as a starter, 4 as a main course

> 7 tablespoons olive oil
>
> 400g monkfish fillets, trimmed and cut into 2–3cm bite-sized pieces
>
> 2 large Spanish onions, finely chopped
>
> 2 green peppers, halved, seeded and finely chopped
>
> 6 garlic cloves, finely chopped
>
> $^1/_2$ teaspoon fennel seeds
>
> 800ml hot Fish Stock (see page 175)
>
> 1 teaspoon (about 100) saffron threads, see page 172
>
> 250g calasparra (paella) rice (see Spanish Suppliers)
>
> 80ml white wine or fino sherry
>
> 1 small bunch fresh flat-leaf parsley, roughly chopped
>
> $^1/_2$ teaspoon sweet smoked Spanish paprika (see page 111)
>
> 225g piquillo peppers, torn in strips
>
> 1 lemon, in wedges
>
> sea salt and black pepper

Heat 2 tablespoons of the olive oil in a 30–40cm paella pan or frying pan over a medium to high heat. Carefully add the monkfish to the pan and stir-fry until still fractionally undercooked in the centre. Pour the monkfish and any of its juices into a bowl and put to one side. Wipe the pan clean with kitchen paper, and put back on the heat. Add the remaining olive oil and when it is hot, the onions and peppers, and cook for 15–20 minutes, stirring every so often. Turn down the heat to medium, add the chopped garlic and fennel seeds, and cook for a further 10 minutes or until the garlic and the onions have some colour and are sweet. Meanwhile bring the stock to the boil and add the saffron to it to infuse for 10 minutes off the heat. Now add the rice to the pan and stir for 1 minute to coat with the vegetables and oil. (Up to now everything can be done in advance, and you need only continue 20 minutes before you wish to eat.)

Put the heat to medium to high, and add the white wine or sherry to the pan, followed by the hot stock. At this point, add half the parsley and the paprika and season perfectly with salt and pepper. Do not stir the rice after this as it affects the channels of stock, which allow the rice to cook evenly. Simmer for 10 minutes or until there is just a little liquid above the rice. Spread the monkfish out evenly over the rice along with its juices. Push each piece of monkfish under the stock. Gently shake the pan to prevent sticking and turn the heat down to medium to low. Cook for 5 more minutes or until there is just a little liquid left at the bottom of the rice. Turn off the heat and cover the pan tightly with foil. Let the rice sit for 3–5 minutes before serving. Decorate with strips of piquillo peppers, the rest of the chopped parsley and the lemon. We would serve this paella with a salad.

PILAVS

Pilafs come in many forms and flavours from Turkey all the way east to India. They are essentially rice steamed with any number of different ingredients. At Moro we cook them to accompany simply cooked meat or fish. If you can follow this basic technique, it will open the door to limitless pilav possibilities. Most of the recipes here are Turkish in origin and therefore called 'pilav' as opposed to 'pilaf'.

The way we wash rice for pilav has an element of ritual about it. Put your rice in a bowl and cover with cold water. Rub the rice with your fingertips until the water becomes cloudy with the starch. Strain off the cloudy water and repeat the process three times (or until the water runs clear). Finally pour off the water, replace with warm water and stir in a teaspoon of salt. The rice is then soaked in the fridge for at least 3 hours. The salt stops the rice from breaking up and the soaking reduces the cooking time by half. We have made successful pilavs without soaking the rice, but a little more water and time is needed when it comes to cooking the rice.

Broad bean and dill pilav

This pilav also works well with peas. If your individual broad beans are longer than 1.5cm, we feel it is necessary to blanch and peel each one, for otherwise they will be unpleasantly tough.

Serves 4

> 75g unsalted butter
> 6 spring onions thinly sliced (with all the green leaves)
> a pinch of ground allspice
> 150g basmati rice, soaked as above
> 500g podded broad beans or 1.5kg in pods
> 1 medium bunch fresh dill, roughly chopped
> 1/2 small bunch fresh flat-leaf parsley, roughly chopped
> sea salt and black pepper

TO SERVE
200g home-made or Greek yoghurt, thinned with 2 tablespoons milk
and seasoned with $1/2$ crushed garlic clove and a pinch of allspice

Over a medium heat melt the butter in a saucepan and fry the spring onion
and allspice for 10 minutes until sweet. Stir the drained rice into the
saucepan and coat with the butter. Add the broad beans and two-thirds of
the chopped dill and parsley and stir in well. Cover the rice by 5mm water
and season with salt and pepper. Lay some damp greaseproof paper on the
water and bring to the boil over a medium to high heat. When it comes to the
boil, put a lid on the pan and cook quite fast for 5 minutes. Now turn down
the heat to medium to low for another 5 minutes before it is ready to serve.
Sprinkle the rest of the dill and parsley on each serving. We serve this rice
with seasoned yoghurt as here, but it is also good with Lamb Kibbeh Cooked
in Yoghurt (see page 208), or roasted or grilled fish.

Saffron rice

Saffron rice is eaten at weddings and on special occasions throughout much of the Muslim world. It is an elegant rice, subtly scented with butter and spice. This dish can be made in 15 minutes if the rice has been soaked.

Serves 4

> 80g unsalted butter
>
> $1/2$ cinnamon stick
>
> 5 whole green cardamom pods, cracked
>
> 3 whole black peppercorns
>
> 200g basmati rice, washed and soaked in salted water for 3 hours
>
> 2 tablespoons roughly chopped pistachio nuts (optional)
>
> 2 tablespoons barberries (optional, see Iranian Suppliers)
>
> 1 good pinch of saffron threads (about 100 threads), infused in 4 tablespoons boiling water (see page 172)
>
> sea salt

> **TO SERVE**
>
> 200g home-made or Greek yoghurt, seasoned with 1 crushed garlic clove, salt and pepper
>
> Caramelised Crispy Onions (see page 172)

Melt the butter in a saucepan over a medium to low heat. Add the cinnamon, cardamom pods and black peppercorns and gently fry the spices until their aromas start to be released, about 4 minutes. Drain the rice well, add it to the butter, and stir to coat for a minute. Turn up the heat to medium to high. If you are using pistachios and/or barberries stir them in now. Pour enough water over the rice to cover it roughly by 1cm, and season with salt. Rest some greaseproof paper on the surface of the water, then place a lid on the pan, bring to the boil and simmer for 5 minutes. Lift the lid and paper off the pan and drizzle the saffron water evenly over the rice. Replace the paper and lid. Turn down the heat to medium to low and cook for another 4–5 minutes.

Serve with the seasoned yoghurt on the side and caramelised crispy onions on top.

Caramelised crispy onions

We slice our peeled and halved onions in a machine with a slicing attachment with a thin blade as this ensures the onions are not only thinly sliced but evenly as well. This also ensures even cooking (as long as you stir the onions regularly).

To caramelise 2 large onions for four, heat 300ml sunflower oil in a large saucepan or frying pan. Unless you have a very large pan it will be necessary to fry the onion in two batches. When hot, add half the sliced onions and cook over a medium heat, stirring occasionally. It is important that the onions fry in a lot of oil otherwise they will not go crispy. When the onions turn golden to mahogany in colour, remove with a slotted spoon and spread out either on a rack or on kitchen paper. Repeat with the remaining onions. When finished, strain the oil and keep it for another recipe, bearing in mind it will taste of onions.

Azafrán
SAFFRON

 'Azafrán' is a Spanish word of Arabic origin, meaning 'yellow'. The area around La Mancha in central Spain produces some of the best-quality saffron in the world. Saffron is the stigma of a variety of lilac crocus called 'Crocus sativus', which comes into flower during the early part of October. The crocus is picked at first light before the flowers open to minimise the risk of damage from the elements. The stigmas are then sorted by hand before being dried and boxed. It takes about 200 crocuses to fill a 1g box, so saffron is a precious commodity. Considering all this, far from being expensive, it actually seems rather cheap. If we had to rely on a florist for our supply of crocuses, it would be a different story. Saffron is highly prized in cooking, particularly in rices and fish stews, for it has a distinctive, earthy flavour that is at the heart of Spanish cooking especially. To use saffron, we warm it over the gentlest of heats until just brittle (saffron varies in dryness), then crumble it roughly, pour boiling water on it to cover, and then leave it to infuse for anything from 10 minutes. Spain produces around 70 per cent of the world's saffron. The rest is from Kashmir and Iran.

Aubergine and tomato pilav

The tomato makes this rice slightly heavier than some, but the textures and tastes are wonderful.

Serves 4

    1 large or 2 small aubergines
    40g butter
    2 tablespoons olive oil
    4 garlic cloves, thinly sliced
    $1/3$ teaspoon ground allspice
    1x 400g tin plum tomatoes, mashed and broken up until smooth
    150g basmati rice, washed and soaked in salted water for 3 hours
    $1/2$ small bunch fresh flat-leaf parsley, roughly chopped
    sea salt and black pepper

To prepare the aubergines, cut off the stalks and then slice each aubergine into 3cm cubes. Toss the aubergine in 1 heaped teaspoon of fine sea salt and leave for 20 minutes in a colander. The salt makes for a far softer and more delicious aubergine later.

Preheat the oven to 230°C/450°F/Gas 8.

Melt the butter and 1 tablespoon of the olive oil in a saucepan large enough to cook the rice in. Gently fry the garlic until light brown, then add the allspice and the tomatoes. Simmer for 20 minutes. Meanwhile shake the aubergines and then dry with kitchen paper. Toss them with the remaining olive oil and spread out on a baking tray. Roast for 15 minutes in the pre-heated oven until golden and soft.

Stir the rice into the tomato and add just enough water to cover the rice by 5mm. Season with a little salt and pepper. Add the roasted aubergines, and cover with greaseproof paper and then a lid. Bring to the boil over a medium to high heat and cook fast for 2 minutes then turn down the heat to medium to low and cook for another 8 minutes. Let the rice sit for 5 minutes before serving with the parsley on top. At Moro we serve this rice with grilled chicken or lamb.

Lamb pilav with cabbage and caraway

This dish, Turkish in origin, is a meal in itself. The caraway is a classic combination with the cabbage.

Serves 4

        2 tablespoons olive oil

        400g stewing lamb, cut in pieces no larger than 1cm square

        1 dessertspoon tomato purée

        ½ medium onion, finely grated

        ½ cinnamon stick

        75g butter

        2 teaspoons caraway seeds

        175g basmati rice, washed and soaked in salted water for 3 hours

        ½ medium white cabbage, about 500g, finely shredded

        1 small bunch fresh flat-leaf parsley, roughly chopped

        sea salt and black pepper

TO SERVE

200g home-made or Greek yoghurt, seasoned with 1 crushed garlic
    clove, a pinch of ground allspice, salt and pepper

1 lemon, cut into wedges

In a saucepan, heat half the olive oil over a medium heat and add the lamb, tomato purée, grated onion and cinnamon, and cover with water. Bring to a gentle simmer, and cook for 30–40 minutes until the lamb is tender. Remove and season with salt and pepper.

In another large saucepan, melt the butter and, when it begins to foam, add the caraway and fry for a minute to release the flavour. Now add the rice, and cook for another minute before adding the lamb and its juices, the cabbage and half the parsley. Add water to bring the level of the liquid to about 1cm above the rice. Cover with greaseproof paper and a lid and steam for 8 minutes. Remove the lid and paper and let the rice sit for another 5 minutes before sprinkling the rest of the parsley on top and serving with a salad, the seasoned yoghurt and wedges of lemon.

Chicken Stock

Makes approx. 2 litres

    2 chicken carcasses, raw or roasted, with giblets if possible

    2 large carrots

    1 large onion, skin on, halved

    1 garlic bulb, broken up roughly

    2 celery sticks

    3 bay leaves, preferably fresh

    1 teaspoon black peppercorns

    a bunch of fresh flat-leaf parsley

    a few fennel seeds (optional)

    sea salt and black pepper

Place all the ingredients except for the salt and pepper in a large saucepan or stockpot and cover with cold water (about 4 litres). Bring to the boil and then turn down the heat to a gentle simmer, skimming off any scum. Simmer for about 1½ –2 hours or until the stock has reduced roughly by half, and has acquired a good smell and colour. Do not boil the stock too fast as this can make it go cloudy. Strain in a chinois or fine-mesh sieve, season with salt and pepper and allow to cool completely. To remove the fat from the top, simply skim off with a ladle or, more effectively, when the stock is cold, put in the fridge or freezer until the fat solidifies.

For a lamb or other meat stock, substitute 1.5kg meat bones for the chicken carcasses, and proceed in exactly the same way.

Fish Stock

Makes approx. 2 litres

    the head (without gills) and bones (about 2 kg) of 1 large white fish

        (turbot, sea bass, brill or cod, ask your fishmonger)

    1 large carrot

    1 large onion, skin on, halved

    1 garlic bulb, broken up roughly

    2 celery sticks

½ x 400g tin whole plum tomatoes, drained of juice

1 fennel bulb, quartered, or 1 teaspoon fennel seeds

3 bay leaves, preferably fresh

1 teaspoon black peppercorns

a bunch of fresh flat-leaf parsley

sea salt and black pepper

Give the fish bones and head a good wash under cold water until the water more or less runs clear, then transfer to a large saucepan and add all the other ingredients except for the salt and pepper. Generously cover with cold water (3 litres). Bring to the boil and then turn down the heat to a gentle simmer, skimming off any scum. Simmer for 15–20 minutes, but no longer, otherwise the stock will not taste fresh. Strain in a chinois or fine-mesh sieve, then season with salt and pepper.

At Moro we talk to our fish suppliers every morning to find out what was landed the night before. Try to keep an open mind when planning what fish to cook, and make your choice according to what is at its best and most recently caught. Although a recipe may specify one fish (often because it is a classic way of serving it), there is always room for flexibility, and where possible we have suggested alternatives.

A lot of fishmongers can get a greater choice than they have on show, and it is up to you to ask if he can get sardines, anchovies or squid ink for example. With personal contact, you are, as it were, only one person away from the sea and the main fish markets of your area. A good fishmonger will tell you what is seasonal, local and good value, and teach you what to look for in a fresh fish – bright, clear eyes, deep-red gills, rigid flesh (rigor mortis), with a good smell of the sea – and they will even prepare the fish how you want it.

Grilled or roasted fish

Most of the fish we serve in the restaurant is cooked very simply, that is, grilled over charcoal or roasted in our wood oven and, like our meat, is served with seasonal vegetables, sometimes a sauce and lemon. As a general guide, we offer about 200-225g per portion of filleted fish, a bit more (about 250g) if on the bone and, if whole, like bream or red mullet, more still (up to 400-500g). Most white fish can be substituted with another (if not sea bass, then monkfish, hake, turbot etc.), and most fish can be grilled or roasted (although hake or cod are definitely better roasted). Always cook fish over a high heat, until just cooked through (the flesh should flake easily), but still juicy inside. Filleted fish takes a shorter time to cook than fish on the bone. Opposite are some of our favourite combinations – some based around Spanish flavours, some rooted in the Muslim Mediterranean – when planning a Moro plate around a piece of grilled or roasted fish. This is by no means a rigid guide, and you should experiment with other recipes in the book that appeal to you, but try not to cross over the cultures.

SPANISH

Roasted beetroot and Almond and Sherry Vinegar Sauce (see page 251)

Escalivada and Alioli (see pages 238 and 248)

Braised spinach and Romesco (see pages 234 and 252)

Cooked judión beans, grilled leeks and Romesco (see pages 113 and 252)

MUSLIM MEDITERRANEAN

Saffron Rice, Tahini Sauce and Chickpea Salad (see pages 170, 255 and 246)

Braised Chard and Tarator (see pages 234 and 256)

Courgettes with Pinenuts and Raisins and Yoghurt and Dill Sauce
    (see pages 243 and 255)

New potatoes, artichokes and Harissa (see page 254)

Fish marinades

Sometimes we marinate fish, but marinades are by no means essential, especially when the fish is extremely fresh. Nor does fish need to marinate for long, as the marinade is not required for tenderising, but to impart a delicate flavour. Below are two simple marinades that we sometimes use for any fish, one Spanish, the other Muslim Mediterranean.

Serves 4

SPANISH MARINADE

2 garlic cloves

1½ teaspoons fresh thyme or oregano

juice of 1 lemon

½ teaspoon sweet smoked Spanish paprika (optional, see page 111)

1 tablespoon olive oil

sea salt and black pepper

Crush the garlic and herbs in a mortar and pestle with a pinch of salt and pepper until smooth. Add the lemon juice and paprika. Rub all over the fish, then drizzle with the olive oil. Leave to marinate in the fridge for 1–2 hours.

MUSLIM MEDITERRANEAN MARINADE

2 garlic cloves

1½ teaspoons freshly ground cumin

juice of 1 lemon

1 tablespoon olive oil

sea salt and black pepper

Crush the garlic and cumin in a mortar and pestle with a pinch of salt and pepper until smooth. Stir in the lemon juice. Rub all over the fish, then drizzle with the olive oil. Leave to marinate in the fridge for 1–2 hours.

Pescado en adobo
MARINATED FRIED FISH

'Adobo' is the Spanish word for marinade, and this Moorish dish is normally served as a tapa in Spain. 'Cazón' or dogfish or huss is usually used (also common in Britain), but if it is unavailable we sometimes use another firm fish such as monkfish, eel or swordfish.

Serves 4

4 x 200-225g dogfish fillets

300ml sunflower oil

6 tablespoons plain flour, seasoned with salt and pepper

1 lemon, quartered

sea salt and black pepper

ADOBO

2 garlic cloves

2 teaspoons cumin seeds

1½ tablespoons red wine vinegar (Cabernet Sauvignon, see Spanish Suppliers)

a pinch of saffron (about 40 strands), infused in 2 tablespoons boiling water (see page 172)

½ teaspoon sweet smoked Spanish paprika (see page 111)

½ small bunch fresh oregano, roughly chopped, or 1 teaspoon dried oregano

½ tablespoon olive oil

For the adobo, crush the garlic and cumin in a mortar and pestle with a pinch of salt until smooth. Then mix the garlic, cumin, vinegar, saffron-infused water, paprika and oregano together in a large bowl. Traditionally the fish is cut into cubes about 3-4cm square, but you can leave the fillets whole and simply add them to the marinade. Mix well, finish off with the olive oil and leave to marinate for at least an hour or two in the fridge, or overnight.

Heat the sunflower oil in a large heavy saucepan. Dust the fish with flour, shaking off any excess. Gently place in the hot oil (in batches if necessary) and fry until golden and cooked through. Drain on kitchen paper, season with a little more salt and serve with wedges of lemon.

Grilled marinated swordfish with sweet tomato sauce

This dish is wonderful for a barbecue and perfect with tuna instead of swordfish. The spiced fish goes well with a tomato sauce subtly flavoured with cinnamon.

Serves 4

    4 swordfish steaks, 2–3cm thick, about 225g each in weight
    Sweet Tomato Sauce (see page 257), cooked with ½ cinnamon stick
    1 lemon, quartered

    MARINADE
    2 garlic cloves
    juice of 1 lemon
    ½ medium onion, grated
    1½ teaspoons sweet smoked Spanish paprika (see page 111)
    1½ teaspoons freshly ground cumin
    1 tablespoon olive oil
    sea salt and black pepper

For the marinade, crush the garlic in a mortar and pestle with a pinch of salt until smooth. Stir in the lemon juice. Transfer to a small bowl and add the onion, paprika and cumin. Rub all over the fish, then drizzle on the olive oil. Leave to marinate in the fridge for at least an hour or two.

Meanwhile prepare the sweet tomato sauce, adding the cinnamon while simmering. If you are grilling the fish over charcoal, light the barbecue three-quarters of an hour before you wish to cook. If you are grilling under a domestic grill turn it to a high heat 5–10 minutes before you are ready to cook or use a very hot griddle pan. Grill the fish for about 2–3 minutes either side until the outside is charred slightly but the flesh is still slightly pink and juicy inside. (If we use tuna instead of swordfish, we like to serve it medium rare to rare.) Serve with the spiced sweet tomato sauce, lemon and a simple pilav (see pages 168–174) and/or salad.

Fish tagine with potatoes, tomatoes and olives

Tagine is the famous Moroccan stew traditionally cooked in an earthenware pot of the same name. The fish is first marinated in charmoula, a classic fish marinade of garlic, cumin, coriander, paprika and lemon. We ate this particular tagine somewhere between Safi and Essaouira.

Serves 4

> 4 hake steaks, about 250g each, or fillets of 225g each (you can use any white fish)
>
> 20 small, waxy new potatoes, peeled (Charlotte, Roseval, Ratte)
>
> 3 tablespoons olive oil
>
> 4 garlic cloves, thinly sliced
>
> 15 cherry tomatoes, halved
>
> 4 green peppers, grilled until black and blistered, skinned, seeded and sliced into strips
>
> a handful of black oily olives
>
> 100ml water
>
> sea salt and black pepper

CHARMOULA

> 2 garlic cloves
>
> 1 level teaspoon sea salt
>
> 2 teaspoons freshly ground cumin
>
> juice of 1 lemon
>
> ½ tablespoon good-quality red wine vinegar
>
> 1 teaspoon paprika
>
> 1 small bunch fresh coriander, roughly chopped
>
> 1 tablespoon olive oil

We make the charmoula in a mortar and pestle. Pound the garlic with the salt until a smooth paste is formed, then add the cumin followed by the lemon juice, vinegar, paprika, coriander and olive oil. Rub two-thirds of the charmoula mixture into the fish and stand in the fridge for between 20 minutes and 2 hours.

Boil the potatoes in salted water for 10–15 minutes until just tender. Drain and halve lengthways. In a medium saucepan, heat 2 tablespoons of the olive oil over a medium heat and fry the garlic until light brown. Add the tomatoes and toss for 2 minutes until they begin to soften. Stir in the green peppers and remaining charmoula and check for seasoning. In a 25cm tagine, saucepan or frying pan with a lid, spread the potatoes evenly over the bottom. Scatter three-quarters of the pepper and tomato mixture over the potatoes, then place the marinated fish on top. Dab a little of the remaining pepper and tomato on top of each fish as well as the olives. Add the water, drizzle on the remaining tablespoon of olive oil, put on the lid and steam over a medium to high heat for 10–15 minutes or until the fish is cooked through. The beauty of this dish is that it hardly needs anything to accompany it, perhaps just a little salad and some bread (see page 20 for Moroccan Bread).

Mero en amarillo
GROUPER WITH PEAS AND SAFFRON

This recipe was given to us by Lidia's mum, Milagros, who usually makes this dish with 'mero', grouper, a popular fish in Spain, but you can replace it with sea bass or hake. Pounding fried bread and garlic is a traditional Spanish method for thickening sauces.

Serves 4

- 3 tablespoons olive oil
- 6 garlic cloves, peeled
- 2 thick slices white bread, crusts removed, cut into small cubes
- 4 thick grouper fillets, skin on (about 225g), or fish steaks (about 250g)
- 150ml white wine
- 60 saffron strands, infused in 5 tablespoons boiling water
- 250g peas, fresh or frozen
- sea salt and black pepper

In a large frying pan heat the olive oil over a medium heat. When the oil is hot, add the garlic and fry gently, turning down the heat if necessary, until golden on all sides. Remove with a slotted spoon and add the bread. When the bread is also golden brown all over, remove the pan from the heat. Transfer both bread and garlic to a mortar and pestle or food processor and pound/pulse to a thick paste.

When you are ready to cook the fish, return the pan to a medium heat, adding a little more oil if necessary. Season the grouper with salt and pepper and, when the oil is hot, place skin-side up in the pan. Fry for 2 minutes until sealed, then turn over with a spatula and fry for a further 3–5 minutes until the skin begins to crisp. Now add the pounded bread and garlic back to the pan along with the white wine. Let the wine bubble for 30 seconds, then add the saffron-infused water and peas. Turn the heat down low and let everything gently simmer together with the lid on until the grouper is cooked through, about 5–10 minutes. Check for seasoning. Serve with some fried potatoes (see page 232) and a salad.

Chocos con papas
CUTTLEFISH WITH POTATOES

For this recipe you can use any size of cuttlefish or squid, for it is braised for as long as is necessary until it becomes tender. This is sometimes given as a tapa in Andalucía with a delicious glass of cold fino.

Serves 4

> 4 small cuttlefish or medium squid (no larger than hand size)
> 4 tablespoons olive oil
> 1 large Spanish onion, roughly chopped
> 3 garlic cloves, thinly sliced
> 3 bay leaves, preferably fresh
> 2 red peppers, seeded and roughly chopped
> 4 medium potatoes, peeled, cut in half and sliced about 1cm thick
> 150ml white wine or fino sherry
> 1 small bunch fresh flat-leaf parsley, roughly chopped
> sea salt and black pepper

To clean the cuttlefish or squid, refer to page 188, then cut into strips about 7cm long and 3cm thick. In a large heavy saucepan, heat the oil over a medium flame. When the oil is hot, add the onion and a pinch of salt. Cook the onion, stirring occasionally, until it begins to turn golden, about 10 minutes, then add the garlic, bay and red pepper. After another 10–15 minutes, or when the onion and pepper mixture is caramelised and sweet, lightly salt the potatoes and add to the pan, along with the cuttlefish (or squid) and white wine. Simmer for 20–30 minutes until tender, adding water when the sauce becomes too thick. Check for seasoning and sprinkle with parsley just before serving.

Tahini

Tahini is an oily paste made from pounded sesame seeds. It has a rich, nutty flavour and is used throughout the Middle East in a variety of ways – as a creamy sauce to go with falafel, fish or vegetables, or in dips such as hummus or baba ghanoush. Tahini comes in light and dark pastes, and does vary considerably in taste. We prefer the paler version, as it is lighter and less strong in flavour. Because of its high oil content, tahini in a closed jar will keep for a year before it starts to taste stale.

Cod baked with tahini sauce

Fish with tahini sauce is a classic Lebanese recipe that has become a Moro favourite. Any white fish goes well with tahini – sea bass, turbot or monkfish are all good alternatives to the cod used here. We serve this dish hot as a main course with saffron rice and chickpea salad, but it can also be served at room temperature as part of a selection of mezze.

Serves 4

    4 thick cod fillets, skin on, about 200g each in weight

    3 tablespoons olive oil

    sea salt and black pepper

    TO SERVE

    Tahini Sauce (see page 255)

    Chickpea Salad (see page 246)

    Saffron Rice (see page 170)

    1 small bunch fresh flat-leaf parsley (optional), roughly chopped

    2 tablespoons pomegranate seeds, or 2 teaspoons nigella seeds (see page 40), optional

    1 lemon, quartered

To start off with, prepare the tahini sauce, chickpea salad and saffron rice as the fish takes no time to cook and you want to be ready with everything else first. Preheat the oven to 220°C/425°F/Gas 7.

To cook the cod, place a frying pan with a heat-resistant handle or a roasting tray over a high heat. Add the olive oil to cover the bottom of the pan. Season the cod well and with one hand carefully place the fish in the pan, skin-side up, whilst shaking the pan with the other hand to prevent the fish from sticking. Cook for 1–2 minutes until sealed. Carefully turn the fish over with a spatula and place in the oven for about 5–8 minutes, or continue on the hob. When cooked, the flesh of the fish should flake easily, and be white all the way through. If it is slightly opaque it might need a little more time. While the fish is still there, pour the tahini sauce into the pan to warm for half a minute. Transfer to warm plates, spooning the sauce over the fish, followed by the parsley (if using), and a few seeds on top. Serve with the chickpea salad, saffron rice and lemon on the side.

Calamares rellenos de Carlos
CARLOS'S STUFFED SQUID

By the very nature of its body, squid is an ideal thing to stuff, and for this reason many recipes for stuffed squid have evolved. This is the one we prefer, given to us by a Spanish friend and chef, Carlos.

Serves 4

    8 medium squid, no larger than hand size

    10 tablespoons olive oil

    1 large Spanish onion, finely diced

    2 garlic cloves, finely chopped

    2 bay leaves, preferably fresh

    200ml fino sherry

    1 large bunch fresh flat-leaf parsley, roughly chopped

    2 hard-boiled eggs, chopped

    50ml water

    sea salt and black pepper

To clean the squid, first pull the head away from the body and with your fingers empty out the body cavity (gut, any ink sac and transparent cuttlebone) and discard. Gently pull the wings free from the sides, being careful not to puncture the body, and remove any pinkish membrane. Rinse clean under running water and drain. Keep the tentacles intact by cutting just above where the tentacles join. Remove the eyes and mouth. Chop up the squid wings and tentacles and set aside.

In a frying pan, heat half the olive oil over a medium heat and fry the onion until golden and sweet, about 15 minutes, stirring occasionally. Add the chopped garlic and bay leaves, and cook for 5 more minutes. Drain the onion mixture from the pan into a sieve and set aside. Return the flavoured oil. Turn up the heat and, when the oil is hot, throw in the chopped wings and tentacles. Fry briskly until lightly cooked, then add half the sherry, stirring all the while. Return the onion mixture to the pan followed by half the parsley. Cook the sauce for a minute until thickened or until the smell or taste of alcohol from the sherry has disappeared, then season, and remove from the heat. Add the chopped egg and remaining parsley to the squid/onion mixture and taste for seasoning. Stuff each squid body two-thirds full with this, but do not overfill since the squid will shrink as it cooks. You can secure the ends shut with toothpicks if you wish.

Take a saucepan that will hold the stuffed squid in a single layer, and heat the remaining olive oil. Lightly brown the squid on all sides, and then add the remainder of the sherry and the water. Cook until the alcohol has burnt off and the squid is tender, shaking the pan occasionally until the sauce has thickened slightly. Taste for seasoning.

We serve this with rocket salad and boiled potatoes, or steamed basmati rice flavoured with coarsely ground coriander seeds.

Calamares en su tinta
SQUID IN ITS OWN INK

The ink in this dish gives a deliciously oily richness and startling appearance, yet the flavour is surprisingly subtle. We have yet to extrude the ink from the squid itself but instead have always bought squid ink sachets from our fishmonger.

Serves 4

> 6–8 medium squid, about the size of a hand
> 1 large Spanish onion, finely chopped
> 1 green pepper, seeded and finely chopped
> 6 tablespoons olive oil
> 3 garlic cloves, finely chopped
> 150ml white wine
> 1 tablespoon tomato purée
> 6 x 4–5g sachets squid or cuttlefish ink (from a fishmonger or good
>   delicatessen)
> sea salt and black pepper

To clean the squid, refer to page 188, then cut the body and wings into strips about 7cm long and 2cm wide, and the tentacles in half. Soften the onion and pepper in half the olive oil over a medium heat for 15–20 minutes, stirring occasionally, until golden and sweet. Turn down the heat if necessary. Now add the chopped garlic and continue cooking for another 5 minutes. Add your white wine, bring to a gentle simmer and reduce by half, followed by the tomato purée and squid ink. Taste for seasoning and set aside.

Put a large frying pan over a high heat, add the rest of the olive oil and when it starts to smoke, add the squid carefully, as it might spit. Keeping the temperature high, stir continuously for a minute before adding the sauce. Bring the sauce to the boil, adding a little water if the sauce is too thick, and cook for 30 seconds or until the squid is just tender. At Moro we serve this dish with Mashed Potato with Garlic (see page 231), watercress salad and piquillo peppers in strips over the squid.

Merluza en salsa verde
HAKE IN SALSA VERDE

Hake in 'salsa verde' (green sauce) is a Basque dish, often served with a few clams, peas and/or white asparagus in the sauce. It is a wonderful dish that can be made at the last minute. This is our version.

Serves 4

> 25g butter
>
> 3 tablespoons olive oil
>
> 4 thick hake steaks, weighing about 250g each
>
> 4 tablespoons plain flour, seasoned with salt and pepper
>
> 3 garlic cloves, finely chopped
>
> ½ teaspoon fennel seeds
>
> 8 tablespoons finely chopped fresh flat-leaf parsley
>
> 100ml white wine
>
> 150ml hot Fish Stock (see page 175)
>
> 350g small clams, venus or palourdes (optional), rinsed
>
> 75g peas, fresh or good-quality frozen
>
> sea salt and black pepper

In a large frying pan over a medium heat, heat the butter and the olive oil. Dust the hake in the seasoned flour, shaking off any excess, and add to the pan when the butter begins to foam. Keep aside ½ tablespoon of the flour. Fry for about 2 minutes until sealed and golden, carefully flip over with a spatula, fry for another 2 minutes, then remove and set aside. Now add the garlic and fennel seeds to the pan, fry until golden, then stir in 5 tablespoons of the parsley. When it turns slightly darker, turn the heat to low and stir in the reserved flour. Cook for half a minute, then whisk in the wine and fish stock, slowly at first. Return the fish to the pan, add the clams (if using) and peas, bring to a gentle simmer, cover and cook for a couple more minutes until the fish is cooked through and the clams are open. Sprinkle on the remaining parsley. This is delicious served with Mashed Potato with Garlic (see page 231) and a watercress salad or braised fennel.

Rape al ajillo
MONKFISH WITH GARLIC AND FINO

The classic Spanish way of cooking meat 'al ajillo' (with lots of garlic and wine) is also delicious with fish, especially monkfish.

Serves 4

    4 tablespoons olive oil
    8 garlic cloves, peeled
    4 trimmed monkfish fillets, about 200–225g each
    150ml fino or manzanilla sherry (see Sherry Suppliers)
    2 bay leaves, preferably fresh
    50 saffron strands, infused in 4 tablespoons boiling water
    100g raisins, soaked in warm water
    100g pinenuts, lightly toasted

In a large, heavy saucepan, heat the oil over a low to medium flame and gently fry the garlic until pale golden all over. Remove with a slotted spoon and set aside. Now turn up the heat and add the monkfish, seasoned with a little salt and pepper. When one side has browned slightly, carefully flip over on to the other side and fry for another minute before adding back the garlic followed by the sherry, bay leaves, saffron-infused water, and drained raisins. Simmer for a few minutes to burn off the alcohol and cook the monkfish through, turning occasionally. Taste for seasoning, and finally add the pinenuts. Serve immediately with braised spinach or boiled new potatoes (our favourites are pink fir apple, Charlotte, Roseval and Anya).

Raya con vinagre de Jerez

ROASTED SKATE WITH CARAMELISED GARLIC
AND SHERRY VINEGAR SAUCE

Caramelised garlic and sherry vinegar sauce is a hot dressing that we use for skate, but it also goes well with grilled lamb. The secret is to fry the garlic until brown (more mahogany than golden), as this gives it a nutty flavour. The other tip is to greatly reduce the vinegar: this softens the astringency while helping to concentrate other flavours.

Serves 4

    4 portion-sized skate wings, about 250g each (or monkfish)
    4 tablespoons olive oil
    ½-1 teaspoon sweet smoked Spanish paprika (page 111)
    1 lemon, quartered
    sea salt and black pepper

    CARAMELISED GARLIC AND SHERRY VINEGAR SAUCE
    5 garlic cloves
    3 tablespoons olive oil
    6 tablespoons sherry vinegar (preferably a good-quality, aged one)
    a pinch of sweet smoked mild Spanish paprika
    sea salt and black pepper

Preheat the oven to 220°C/425°F/Gas 7.

For the sauce, slice each garlic clove lengthways and then slice each slice lengthways again to make thin matchsticks. Over a low to medium heat, heat the olive oil in a small saucepan and fry your garlic until it is dark nutty brown in colour. Now add the vinegar and paprika. Bring to the boil and reduce by half. Season well with salt and pepper.

Heat a large metal roasting tin on the hob until very hot. Season the skate with salt and pepper on both sides, drizzle the olive oil into the pan to cover the bottom, and gently ease each wing into the pan, shaking the pan as you do so to prevent the skate from sticking. Place in the oven for about 10 minutes, depending on the thickness of the wing, or until cooked through. Remove and serve immediately with the warm sauce spooned over the fish and a generous sprinkling of paprika. Serve with fried potatoes (see page 232), rocket salad and the lemon.

Vinagre de Jerez
SHERRY VINEGAR

 Sherry vinegar is one of our favourite Spanish ingredients. A good, aged sherry vinegar has more of a distinctive character than other wine vinegars in that it has warmth and nuttiness from being aged in casks, and complexity from being blended in the same way that sherry is blended (i.e., in the solera system, see page 34). The older the blend of sherry vinegar, the more concentrated and complex the flavour (we were once given a 120-year-old vinegar, which was quite extraordinary). When choosing a sherry vinegar, always try to buy one that has been aged, such as the ten-year-old Valdespino brand (see Suppliers).

Romesco de peix
FISH STEW WITH PEPPERS, ALMONDS AND SAFFRON

This is a Catalan fish stew, named after the famous Romesco (nut) sauce from the same region (see page 252). Any combination of fish may be used for this stew: we like monkfish and clams, but mussels, prawns and other firm fish may be substituted or included.

Serves 4

6 tablespoons olive oil

1 large Spanish onion, roughly chopped

2 garlic cloves, thinly sliced

2 dessertspoons finely chopped fresh rosemary

3 bay leaves, preferably fresh

2 red peppers, quartered, seeded and thinly sliced

½ teaspoon sweet smoked Spanish paprika (see page 111)

1 x 400g tin plum tomatoes, drained of juice and roughly chopped

150ml white wine

100ml hot Fish Stock (see page 175)

50 saffron strands, infused in 4 tablespoons boiling water

150g whole blanched almonds, lightly toasted and roughly ground
650g monkfish fillets, cut into chunks about 5cm square
500g clams, venus or palourdes, rinsed
sea salt and black pepper

In a large saucepan or terracotta 'cazuela' (dish), heat the oil over a medium heat. Add the onion and a pinch of salt, and cook the onion, stirring occasionally, until golden and sweet, about 15–20 minutes. Now add the garlic, rosemary, bay and red pepper. When the pepper has softened for at least 10 minutes, add the paprika and tomatoes. Simmer for another 10 minutes, then add the white wine and allow the alcohol to bubble away for a couple of minutes before adding the fish stock and the saffron-infused water. Finally thicken the base with the almonds and taste for seasoning.

When you are almost ready to eat, add the monkfish and clams, put the lid on and simmer until the fish is cooked through and the clams have steamed open (about 5 minutes). Serve with new potatoes and/or a raw fennel salad.

Caballa con pimentón y ajo
BUTTERFLIED MACKEREL WITH PAPRIKA AND GARLIC

Mackerel are still plentiful in Britain and may one day be the only fish it is legal to catch. It is essential to source really fresh fish, and although this can be said about any fish, it is especially important with mackerel as the quality changes more noticeably than most. We ate this dish in a small restaurant in a back street in Barcelona and we will never forget how something so simple can be so exquisite. The raw garlic cut through the oiliness of the mackerel while the paprika gave it an unusual smoky aroma. We now mythologise this restaurant which, sadly, we have never found again!

Serves 4

    3 tablespoons olive oil
    4 portion-sized mackerel, gutted, butterflied (see right and below) or
        filleted (ask your fishmonger)
    3 garlic cloves, very finely chopped
    1 medium bunch fresh flat-leaf parsley, roughly chopped
    2 teaspoons sweet smoked Spanish paprika (see page 111)
    1 lemon, quartered
    sea salt and black pepper

Preheat the oven to 220°C/425°F/Gas 7.

To butterfly a gutted mackerel (or sardine), place on a board and, working from the inside of the belly, run the knife either side of the backbone cutting through the fine bones. Gently pull the backbone away, trying not to take too much flesh with it, then open out the fish, flesh-side up, and remove any large bones on the side of each fillet. Pat the fish dry with kitchen paper.

Place a large roasting tin big enough to accommodate the four butterflied mackerel (or eight fillets) on the hob over a high heat. Drizzle a little oil over the bottom and slide in the fish. Season with salt and pepper and place in the oven for about 8-10 minutes until cooked through. Remove, immediately plate up the fish and sprinkle the chopped garlic, parsley and paprika liberally on top. Serve with lemon and something simple like braised spinach (see page 234) and boiled potatoes with lemon and olive oil. The mackerel may also be grilled or pan-roasted over a high heat for a couple of minutes on each side.

Atún con oloroso
TUNA WITH OLOROSO

This is a version of 'atún encebollado' (tuna with sweet onions), a recipe given to us by Miguel Valdespino of the famous Valdespino sherry bodega in Jerez. The tuna caught off the Atlantic coast of southern Spain is among the best in the world and huge slabs of it, sometimes whole fish, appear in the local fish markets of Jerez and Cádiz during the season. Look out for deep red/purple shiny, firm flesh and do not compromise with the often grey, dull, flabby cuts that certain supermarkets dare to offer.

Serves 4

> 4 thick tuna steaks, about 200–225g each
> 1 garlic clove, crushed to a paste with salt
> 200ml medium-dry oloroso sherry (see Sherry Suppliers)
> 3–4 tablespoons olive oil
> 3 large Spanish onions, thinly sliced
> ½ small bunch fresh flat-leaf parsley, roughly chopped
> 1 lemon, quartered
> sea salt and black pepper

First marinate the tuna. Place the tuna in a dish and rub the garlic all over. Pour over a third of the sherry and leave to sit for an hour in the fridge before cooking.

Meanwhile, place a large frying pan over a medium heat and add the olive oil. When hot, add the onion and a pinch of salt. When the onions have wilted, turn down the heat and continue to cook for a good 20–30 minutes, stirring occasionally, until they are golden brown and sweet in smell and taste. Pour off any excess oil, add the remaining sherry, and simmer until the alcohol has evaporated and you have a nutty, rich sauce. Set aside.

When ready to cook the tuna, heat a clean frying pan until very hot. Add a drizzle of oil followed by the seasoned tuna, and fry briefly on both sides, depending on how rare you like it and the thickness of the cut. When almost cooked, add both the marinade and the onion sauce to the pan to warm through. You could use a griddle pan instead and warm the sauce separately. Serve immediately with the parsley sprinkled on top and the lemon.

Besugo en salazón
BREAM BAKED IN SALT

Baking fish in salt is one of the all-time classic ways of cooking fish throughout the Mediterranean. The Spanish are very fond of baking bream in salt, but any fish can be successfully baked in this way - cod, sea bass, turbot or salmon. This is traditionally served with Alioli (see page 248).

Serves 4

>   4 portion-sized whole bream (red, golden or black), scaled and gutted and trimmed of fins and tail
>   a few parsley stalks
>   1 teaspoon fennel seeds, or 1 fennel bulb, roughly chopped
>   1 lemon, sliced
>   3 kg rock sea salt

Preheat the oven to 220°C/425°F/Gas 7.

Stuff the parsley stalks, fennel or fennel seeds and lemon inside the cavity of each fish.

Cover the bottom of a large, deep roasting tray with half the salt and lay the bream on top. Cover with the remaining salt so the fish are completely covered. Generously sprinkle with water all over the surface as this will help form a strong salt crust, which will encase the fish as it cooks. Place in the oven for 10–15 minutes. Slide a metal skewer into the thick part of the fillet. If the skewer is hot, the fish is ready. Remove from the oven, let it rest for a couple of minutes, then crack open the crust and remove every bit of salt from the fish. Transfer the fish on to a board or plate and remove the skin. Serve warm with Alioli or mayonnaise and Escalivada (see pages 248 and 238), or on a hot day, at room temperature.

MEAT MAIN
COURSES

Most of the meat we serve at Moro is cooked very simply, that is, grilled or roasted. However, what makes it special are the marinades that lend character and tenderness, the charcoal grill and wood oven for a traditional, authentic flavour and the carefully thought-out vegetables to complement each plate. Like all simple ingredients that are not interfered with too much, it is very important they are of the best quality, especially when it comes to meat, which can be tasteless otherwise. We use organic or free-range meat whenever possible, and often particular breeds. We also spend time sourcing small producers who personally rear and understand the benefit of hanging the meat they supply. Our customers often speak highly of our meat, and we believe that details like these make the difference.

LAMB

When we have a piece of lamb we tend to grill it on our charcoal grill as this produces the best flavour. We use leg of lamb that is first boned, then butterflied (see below). Sometimes we cut up this meat, skewer it and then grill it.

Butterflied lamb

We imagine the expressions 'to butterfly' or 'butterflied' must come from scoring a piece of meat or fish to open it out as if it were a butterfly wing. The object is to allow a large piece of meat (or fish) to cook quicker and more evenly, and to give greater surface area for a marinade to have effect.

Serves 4

> 1 leg of spring lamb, weighing about 1.5–1.8 kg
> marinade of choice (see opposite and page 204)

Remove all skin and fat from the leg and bone it. Open out the meat with a knife so it is more or less the same thickness throughout, divide into four pieces, and trim again if necessary. Better still, ask your butcher to do it for you. Alternatively, chops or fillet work just as well, without the bother of too much preparation – only the quantities and cooking time will vary a little.

Place the prepared lamb in a shallow dish, mix all the ingredients of the chosen marinade except for the olive oil (if the marinade calls for it) and rub all over the lamb. This is because oil can prevent the acidity of the lemon juice or vinegar from penetrating the meat. When the other ingredients are rubbed in well, pour on the olive oil and leave the lamb to marinate for a minimum of 1 hour, turning occasionally, or in the fridge overnight so the flavours really get into the meat.

When you are ready to cook, season the lamb well. Place under a hot grill, or on a smoking griddle pan or barbecue, for about 5–8 minutes either side for pink, turning once or twice. Remove and rest for a few minutes before serving. If making kebabs, thread lamb on to skewers about 25cm long, about six to seven pieces per skewer. Grill for the same length of time.

Alternatively, leave the trimmed, flattened leg whole. Grill it slowly on a barbecue until sealed on all sides (or seal in a roasting tin on the hob) and finish it off in a hot oven (220°C/425°F/Gas 7) for approximately 15–20 minutes or until pink. Rest, covered, for 10 minutes before slicing.

Lamb marinades

We always marinate lamb as it helps to tenderise the meat and give it a wonderful flavour. Below are three different marinades, which we use depending on what we are serving with the lamb.

SPANISH MARINADE
2 garlic cloves, crushed to a paste
1 teaspoon sweet smoked Spanish paprika (see page 111)
2 tablespoons red wine vinegar, or juice of 1 lemon
2 teaspoons fresh thyme leaves, finely chopped or pounded
1 tablespoon olive oil
black pepper

SPANISH SUGGESTIONS TO GO WITH LAMB
Spinach and Jerusalem Artichoke Salad (see page 237) and Romesco (see page 252), Patatas a lo Pobre (see page 230), Escalivada (see page 238)

MUSLIM MEDITERRANEAN MARINADE
2 garlic cloves, crushed to a paste

juice of 1 lemon

1 teaspoon tomato purée

2 teaspoons cumin seeds, roughly ground

2 tablespoons roughly chopped fresh coriander

1 tablespoon olive oil

½ onion, finely grated

black pepper

MUSLIM MEDITERRANEAN SUGGESTIONS TO GO WITH LAMB
Tabbouleh and Pistachio Sauce (see pages 45 and 257), Aubergine and Red Pepper Salad with Caramelised Butter and Yoghurt (see page 151), Tomato and Aubergine Pilav (see page 173)

YOGHURT MARINADE
The yoghurt marinade is also good for skewered lamb cut into 3–4cm pieces.

2 garlic cloves, crushed to a paste

1 teaspoon cumin seeds, roughly ground

1 teaspoon sweet smoked Spanish paprika (see page 111)

juice of 1 lemon

40 saffron threads, infused in 3 tablespoons boiling water

½ small onion, finely grated

100g home-made or Greek yoghurt

black pepper

SUGGESTIONS TO GO WITH LAMB SKEWERS
Chickpea Salad, Saffron Rice, Yoghurt and Pomegranate Sauce (see pages 246, 170 and 255), Turnips with Vinegar, Freekeh, Yoghurt and Cumin Sauce (see pages 242, 218 and 133), Turlu Turlu (see page 240)

See Butterflied Lamb (page 203) for marinating instructions.

Roast shoulder of lamb stuffed with saffron rice

This classic dish is a bit of a wow as it looks impressive and the flavours are beautifully evocative.

Serves 4-6

     Saffron Rice (see page 170)

     1 shoulder of lamb, about 1.6-1.8 kg, boned and trimmed of most
         skin and fat

     3 tablespoons olive oil

     75ml water

     4 tablespoons orange-blossom water (see page 274), or finely grated
         zest and juice of 1 orange

     sea salt and black pepper

TO SERVE

Blanched and Braised Chard or braised spinach (see page 234)

200g home-made or Greek yoghurt, thinned with 2 tablespoons milk, with ½ crushed garlic clove and a good pinch of salt

First cook the saffron rice (see page 170) and set aside.

Preheat the oven to 220°C/425°F/Gas 7.

Place the shoulder, skin-side down, on a board and open out fully. Put half, or as much as will fit, of the saffron rice into all the pockets of the boned lamb, roll up and tie with string. Place a large roasting tray on the hob, over a medium heat, add the olive oil and brown all sides of the lamb until sealed. Season the lamb with salt and pepper and place in the oven and roast for about 1–1½ hours or until the meat is pink inside. Remove, transfer the lamb to a board and let it rest for 10 minutes loosely covered with foil.

Meanwhile, make the gravy. Pour off any fat and return the roasting tray to the hob and heat over a medium heat. Add the water and orange-blossom water (or zest and juice) and bring to a gentle simmer, scraping the meat juices off the bottom of the pan. Taste for seasoning, transfer to a small saucepan or bowl and keep hot. When you are ready to eat, slice the lamb and serve with the orange-blossom gravy over the top, the rest of the saffron rice (warmed) on the side, some braised chard or spinach and a little yoghurt.

Cordero con alcachofas y hierbabuena

SLOW-COOKED LAMB WITH ARTICHOKES AND MINT

Artichokes, lamb and mint all go excellently together, and the addition of the oloroso gives depth and richness.

Serves 6

 6 tablespoons olive oil

 1 medium onion, finely chopped

 8 small or 4 large globe artichokes

 juice of ½ lemon

 1.5–1.8 kg neck of lamb, cut into thick pieces, trimmed of skin and fat

 2 tablespoons plain flour, seasoned with salt and pepper

 3 garlic cloves, finely chopped

 1 teaspoon chopped fresh thyme leaves (if dried use ½ teaspoon)

 175ml dry to medium dry oloroso or amontillado sherry

 3 bay leaves, preferably fresh

 5 medium potatoes, quartered

 1 small bunch fresh mint, roughly chopped

 sea salt and black pepper

In a medium saucepan, heat half the olive oil over a medium heat and add the onion. Cook for about 15 minutes, stirring occasionally, until the onion has turned golden and is sweet. Drain and discard the onion oil and put the onion to one side. Meanwhile prepare the artichokes, following the instructions on page 122. Cut each artichoke into quarters or sixths depending on size, and leave in water with the lemon juice until required.

Put a large saucepan over a medium heat, and add the remaining olive oil. Dust the lamb with the flour, and add to the oil when hot. Brown on both sides, then add the garlic and thyme and fry for 30 seconds. Reduce the heat to low, add the sherry and simmer for 2 minutes. Add the onion and bay leaves and enough water to cover the meat generously (1–1.5 litres). Season with salt and pepper and simmer gently with the lid half on for 1½–2 hours until the meat begins to fall off the bone. About 20 minutes before the end of the cooking time, add the potatoes and artichokes. When tender, add the mint and check for seasoning again.

Lamb kibbeh cooked in yoghurt

Kibbehs are a classic throughout the Middle East, particularly in Lebanon and Syria. Although there are many variations, they usually consist of an oval outer casing of ground lamb and bulgur with a stuffing of spiced lamb and pinenuts inside. Shaping kibbeh requires practice – the traditional way (we tell our chefs in the restaurant) is to imagine the shape made when someone puts their hands together in prayer. This is a slightly more unusual recipe in which the kibbeh are cooked in yoghurt.

Serves 4 (makes about 12 kibbeh)

CASING
250g very lean lamb, minced twice
½ small onion, finely grated
2-3 tablespoons water
125g fine bulgur wheat, washed briefly and drained (see Lebanese and Turkish Suppliers)
sea salt and black pepper

STUFFING
½ small onion, finely chopped
2 tablespoons olive oil
150g very lean lamb, minced
¾ teaspoon ground cinnamon
½ teaspoon ground allspice
2 tablespoons water
2-3 tablespoons pinenuts, lightly toasted
1 small bunch fresh coriander, roughly chopped
½ small bunch fresh flat-leaf parsley, roughly chopped
sea salt and black pepper

YOGHURT SAUCE

1 egg or 2 egg yolks

1 level tablespoon cornflour or plain flour

500g home-made or Greek yoghurt, thinned with 3 tablespoons milk

150ml water, lamb stock or Chicken Stock (see page 175)

1 rounded teaspoon dried mint

Caramelised Butter (see page 70)

sea salt and black pepper

TO COOK

3 tablespoons olive oil

To make the casing, put the lamb in a food processor with the onion, salt and pepper, and turn on the machine. Add the water until a smooth paste is formed. Transfer to a bowl, mix in the bulgur and check for seasoning. Chill in the fridge for 20 minutes before using.

To make the stuffing, fry the onion in the olive oil over a medium heat for about 15 minutes until sweet and caramelised. Turn up the heat, add the lamb, cinnamon and allspice, and stir well, breaking up the lamb with the back of a fork, for 2 minutes. Add the water and a pinch of salt and simmer until the water has more or less evaporated. Remove from the heat, stir in the pinenuts, coriander and parsley and check for seasoning.

To form the kibbeh, wet your hands and take a lump of the casing, the size of a golfball, and roll into an oval shape. Make a hole in one end and gently thin it out to no more than 5mm thick. If it cracks, smooth over with a little water. Now the kibbeh is ready for stuffing. Fill the hole with 1–2 teaspoons stuffing, close up the hole and mould back to an oval shape, but this time whole, until it resembles a small egg, only with ends that taper in a more exaggerated way. Set aside.

To make the yoghurt sauce, in a large bowl whisk the egg with the flour until a smooth paste is formed. This will stabilise the yoghurt when it is heated later. Now stir in the yoghurt and thin with the water or stock. Add the dried mint and caramelised butter, and season.

When you are ready to eat, fry the kibbeh in hot olive oil until brown on all sides. Remove from the heat and drain off the oil. Stir in the stabilised yoghurt, return to the heat and warm through until it just begins to bubble. We serve this with Broad Bean and Dill Pilav (see page 168) and extra herbs on top.

PORK

Customers often rave about the pork in the restaurant and as it is Spain's most popular meat, we almost always have it on the menu. Perhaps more than any other meat, it is really important to use good-quality pork, for the difference is staggering when you come to cook it. Normal pork can be very flabby, watery and tasteless, whereas an organic or free-range cut is leaner, drier and has much more flavour. We also try to use specific breeds such as Middle White or Gloucester Old Spot which are known for their flavour and texture.

Cerdo al horno
ROASTED PORK BELLY WITH FENNEL SEEDS

Roast pork with fennel seeds is one of those magical combinations, and our customers adore it. Pork belly is an underestimated cut – it is cheap to buy and when cooked well can be exquisite, but you can use pork loin if you prefer. Ask your butcher to score the skin of the belly, or do it yourself with a Stanley knife (the cuts should be no more than 1cm apart and be deep enough to cut through the rind to form crackling).

Serves 4-6

> 1.5 kg organic or free-range pork belly in one piece, skin on and
>   scored
> 2 garlic cloves, crushed with a pinch of salt
> 1 tablespoon ground fennel seeds
> 1 tablespoon olive oil
> 150ml fino sherry or white wine
> a splash of water (optional)
> sea salt and black pepper

Mix the garlic with the fennel seeds and rub over the flesh of the belly. Place on a large board, skin-side up, and dry the skin thoroughly. Generously sprinkle with fine sea salt (about 1 tablespoon) all over the scored skin. Leave for half an hour, then dust off excess salt.

Preheat the oven to 230°C/450°F/Gas 8.

Transfer the pork to a large roasting tin greased with the olive oil and place in the hot oven on the top shelf. It is important that the oven is really hot to start with, as this intense heat is required to blister the skin and turn it into crackling. Roast at this high heat for a good 30 minutes until hard crackling has formed, then turn the heat down to 190°C/375°F/Gas 5 and transfer to a clean roasting tin. Continue cooking for another 2-2½ hours (35 minutes if loin) until the meat is soft and tender. Remove from the oven, transfer to a chopping board and leave to rest, loosely covered with foil to keep warm, for 15 minutes.

Meanwhile, make the gravy. Pour off any excess oil, and place the roasting tray on the hob on a low to medium heat. Deglaze with the sherry or white wine, scraping the juices off the bottom of the pan as you go. Simmer for a couple of minutes to reduce the alcohol, then taste for seasoning. If it tastes too strong, add a splash of water. Keep hot. To serve the pork we often take it off any ribs beforehand as it is easier to slice.

We like roast pork with one of the following dishes: Patatas a lo Pobre (see page 230), Peas and Potatoes with Anis (see page 229), Quince Alioli (see page 249) and roast vegetables such as potatoes, carrots, celeriac, parsnips or whatever combination you prefer.

Lomo con leche
PORK COOKED IN MILK WITH BAY AND CINNAMON

Pork cooked in milk was one of our favourite dishes to cook at the River Cafe, so we were thrilled when we saw a similar recipe for it in a Spanish book using cinnamon and bay instead of lemon zest and sage.

Serves 4-6

1-1.5 kg boned organic or free-range pork loin, with skin removed

½ teaspoon chopped fresh thyme leaves, or a pinch of dried thyme

4 tablespoons olive oil

½ cinnamon stick

3 bay leaves, preferably fresh

1.5 litres milk

sea salt and black pepper

Trim the pork of excess fat and rub all over with salt, pepper and thyme. Place a large, heavy saucepan over a medium heat and add the olive oil. When the oil is hot, but not smoking, add the pork and seal until golden brown on all sides, but not too dark. Pour off any excess oil, add the cinnamon, bay and milk and bring to a gentle simmer, turning down the heat if necessary. Cook slowly with the lid half off for about 1–1½ hours, turning the meat occasionally, or until the meat is cooked through, but still juicy and tender, making sure it does not catch on the bottom. The milk should have reduced into caramelised, nutty nuggets, and made a wonderful sauce subtly flavoured with cinnamon and bay. If it needs more time to reduce, remove the meat until the sauce is ready. Taste for seasoning. Let the meat relax for 5 minutes before slicing.

We serve this with Mashed Potato with Garlic (see page 231), some rocket or braised spinach (see page 234), and piquillo peppers fried in olive oil and garlic for colour.

Costillas con setas

SLOW-COOKED PORK RIBS WITH MUSHROOMS, FINO AND ROSEMARY

The pork should be nearly falling off the bone in this wonderfully rich, autumnal dish. If you can get hold of chanterelle mushrooms (August to November), it makes the dish look particularly handsome.

Serves 4

> 500g fresh, flat field mushrooms
>
> 500g fresh wild mushrooms such as chanterelles, trompettes de mort, porcini, pieds de mouton
>
> 6 tablespoons olive oil
>
> 1 tablespoon dried porcini mushrooms, covered with 75ml boiling water
>
> 1.5 kg organic or free-range pork belly ribs (the Chinese type)
>
> 2 garlic cloves, finely chopped
>
> 1 teaspoon finely chopped fresh rosemary
>
> 200ml fino sherry
>
> 200ml water
>
> sea salt and black pepper

First pick over the fresh mushrooms for any bits. If they are particularly dirty, wipe them with a damp cloth. Slice the mushrooms up roughly. In a large frying pan over a medium heat, add half the olive oil and when it is hot, the fresh mushrooms. Stir well and cook for 10 minutes or until soft. Season with salt and pepper, drain off any excess oil and set aside.

Meanwhile in a large, heavy saucepan, heat the remaining olive oil over a high heat and add the pork ribs (in batches if necessary). Season and seal until golden on all sides, then remove and set aside. In the same pan, but over a medium heat add the garlic and rosemary and fry until the garlic turns golden. Quickly add the dried porcini and their juice, the sherry, water and the ribs. Loosely cover with baking paper and simmer over a low heat with the lid half on for 1½-2 hours or until the ribs are tender. You may need to add more water. Stir in the fresh mushrooms, cook for another 5 minutes and taste for seasoning.

Migas

Every bread-loving country worth its salt has devised a way of using old bread. Migas is Spain's; bread sauce or bread and butter pudding must be England's. In this time of mass consumerism, using old bread can be surprisingly satisfying. 'Migas', which literally means breadcrumbs, in its simplest (and more authentic) form is bread fried with pork fat. This more complex version with morcilla (blood sausage) makes for a hearty lunch.

Serves 4

500g old white bread (yeast or sourdough), crusts removed, cut in 2cm cubes

2 ñoras peppers (see page 163)

a large pinch (about 60) saffron threads (see page 172)

100ml boiling water

100g manteca (pork fat) or jamón fat (optional)

3 tablespoons olive oil

100g panceta (cured pork belly), smoked or unsmoked, or streaky bacon, cut into thick matchsticks

1 mild onion, finely chopped

3 garlic cloves, thinly sliced

2 green peppers, halved, seeded and roughly chopped

1 teaspoon sweet smoked Spanish paprika (see page 111)

120g morcilla, cut into 1.5cm rounds (see page 114)

TO SERVE

4 fried or poached eggs

white grapes or pomegranate seeds (optional)

Preheat the oven to 200°C/400°F/Gas 6.

Try to use a denser, more rustic style of bread to make migas, but if it is not possible, sprinkle lightly salted water (about 100ml) over pieces of commercial white aerated bread and leave to soak for 10 minutes. Then gently squeeze the bread between your hands to make more chewy, denser crumbs.

Seed and break up the ñoras peppers into small pieces. Put in a bowl with the saffron, cover with the boiling water and leave to infuse. If using manteca (pork fat) or jamón fat, add to the olive oil in a medium saucepan over a low heat, and fry for 5 minutes to melt. Remove the remaining pieces of fat and discard. Now start frying the panceta over a medium heat in the olive oil until it starts to brown, then add the onion, garlic and green pepper and cook for 10 minutes, stirring regularly. If you are not using manteca, simply fry the panceta straightaway over a medium heat in the olive oil, adding the onion etc. as described before.

Turn the heat down to low, add the paprika and continue to soften and lightly caramelise for 15–20 minutes. Lift out the soaking ñoras peppers from the saffron water and stir them into the onion mixture. Place the bread on a baking tray and sprinkle over the saffron water. Now spoon over the panceta-onion mixture, and stir around. Add the pieces of morcilla, then bake in the oven for 20–30 minutes or until crisp, stirring twice.

Traditionally offered with a fried egg, we serve this with a poached egg and some grapes or pomegranate seeds on top.

CHICKEN AND OTHER BIRDS

Like pork, chicken benefits greatly from being organic or free-range, as it is better in both flavour and texture. At Moro most of our chicken is boned, then simply grilled or roasted, although you can leave yours whole. Chicken also lends itself to being marinated with the same marinades as for lamb (see pages 203-4). For skewers, make sure each skewer has some white and some brown meat.

As regards quantity of boned chicken for grilling or roasting, we generally allow a small chicken for two people, one large chicken for four.

BONING THE CHICKEN

Place the chicken on a board and run a sharp knife along one side of the breastbone, working your knife as close as possible down the carcass until you reach the leg. Pull the leg out of its joint so it lies flat and cut around the socket so the half chicken comes away from the carcass. Repeat with the other side. Remove the wing tip and bones from inside the leg by tracing the knife along the leg bones, skin-side down, and extracting them without causing too much damage to the skin.

GRILLING OR ROASTING BONED CHICKEN

When you are ready, season the chicken and place under a medium grill, on a griddle pan or low barbecue for about 10-15 minutes either side, turning once or twice until cooked through and juicy, and the skin is crisp. Remove and allow to rest for a few minutes before serving.

Alternatively, over a medium heat, seal skin-side down in an ovenproof frying pan with a little olive oil, turn over, season and transfer to a hot oven at 230°C/450°F/Gas 8 for about 15 minutes or until cooked. Rest for 5 minutes before slicing. With the roasted chicken, you can make a gravy by adding water to the juices at the bottom of the pan. To roast a whole chicken, see opposite.

SPANISH SUGGESTIONS TO GO WITH GRILLED/ROASTED CHICKEN

Patatas Bravas (see page 232) and salad, Blanched and Braised Chard (or spinach) with added pinenuts and raisins (see page 234), Chickpeas and Spinach (see page 138)

MUSLIM MEDITERRANEAN SUGGESTIONS TO GO WITH
    GRILLED/ROASTED CHICKEN
Green Beans with Cinnamon and Yoghurt (see page 239), Beetroot with
Yoghurt (see page 40), Tabbouleh and Pistachio Sauce (see pages 45 and 257)

Roast chicken with harissa

We ate roast chicken with harissa in Casablanca and, simple as it is, it is
really delicious and a nice change from normal roast chicken.

Serves 4
> 1 medium chicken, organic or free-range, about 1.5 kg, whole
> Harissa (see page 254)
> a little olive oil
> 100ml water
> a squeeze of lemon
> sea salt and black pepper

Rub enough harissa to generously cover the chicken all over, season with salt
and pepper and leave in the fridge for a few hours.

Preheat the oven to 220°C/425°F/Gas 7.

Place the chicken in a lightly oiled roasting tin and pop in the hot oven
to roast for about an hour, basting every now and then. After about 50 minutes, test the leg with a skewer. If the juices run clear, the chicken is cooked;
if they are still pink, it will require a little more time. Transfer the chicken
to a board and leave to rest for 10 minutes, loosely covered in foil.

Meanwhile, make a simple gravy. Pour off most of the oil from the pan,
add the water and a squeeze of lemon, scraping off the juices as you go.
Serve with fried potatoes (see page 232), salad and, of course, more harissa!

Poached chicken with freekeh and spices

In this Lebanese dish, chicken is simmered in spices and served with freekeh, a roasted green wheat that is a staple of Lebanon and Syria especially, and now one of our favourites. The wheat is harvested while the grain is still young (green), then roasted over wood fires or charcoal directly in the fields to burn off the husks. This process gives the wheat a wonderful, earthy, smoky flavour. Freekeh is also delicious with fish and can be cooked with water or stock. This is a clean-tasting and wholesome dish.

Serves 4

1 medium chicken, organic or free-range, about 1.5 kg

1 onion, skin on, halved

1 cinnamon stick

1 teaspoon allspice berries

1 teaspoon black peppercorns

½ bunch fresh flat-leaf parsley

2 medium carrots, quartered

sea salt and black pepper

FREEKEH

200g freekeh (see Lebanese Suppliers)

600ml stock from cooking the chicken

25g butter

½ cinnamon stick

½ small bunch each of fresh flat-leaf parsley, coriander and mint, roughly chopped

a squeeze of lemon

1 tablespoon olive oil

TO SERVE

Blanched and Braised Chard (or spinach, see page 234)

200g home-made or Greek yoghurt thinned with 2 tablespoons milk, seasoned with ½ crushed garlic clove

1 teaspoon sumac (optional, see page 155)

Rinse the chicken, place in a large saucepan and cover generously with cold water, by 5cm at least. Set over a medium heat, add the onion, the cinnamon, allspice, black peppercorns and the parsley. When the water comes to the boil, reduce the heat to a gentle simmer, skimming off any scum as it builds up. Cook the chicken for 45–60 minutes, adding the carrots in the last 10 minutes of cooking. When the chicken is cooked, juicy and tender, turn off the heat, season the stock well with salt and pepper, and allow to rest for 5 minutes.

Meanwhile, prepare the freekeh. Place in a fine-mesh sieve and wash under cold water for 5 minutes to rinse off any dust and dirt. Leave to drain. When the chicken has simmered for half an hour, ladle off 600ml of the stock that has been made. In another saucepan, melt the butter, add the cinnamon stick and fry for a couple of minutes until the butter begins to turn golden. Add the freekeh, and stir well, followed by the stock. Bring to a gentle simmer and cook for about 20 minutes until the freekeh no longer has any bite. Remove from the heat, put on a lid and set aside. When you are ready to serve, warm the freekeh if necessary, stir in the herbs, add a little more stock to moisten it, the squeeze of lemon and olive oil, and check for seasoning.

Serve a slice of brown meat and one of white with the carrots, braised chard or spinach, freekeh and seasoned yoghurt on the side. Pour a small ladle of the hot stock all over and add a sprinkling of sumac.

Pollo al ajillo

CHICKEN COOKED WITH BAY, GARLIC AND WHITE WINE

This is one of Spain's most classic ways of cooking chicken – with lots of garlic, bay and wine – and our favourite. The art of this dish is to try to make the juices of the chicken and the white wine emulsify with the garlicky olive oil.

Serves 4

- 1 medium organic or free-range chicken, about 1.5 kg, jointed into 8 pieces, skin on breast and wings, skin off legs and thighs
- 4 tablespoons olive oil
- 2 garlic bulbs, cloves separated, skins on
- 6 bay leaves, preferably fresh
- 200ml white wine or fino sherry
- 100ml water
- sea salt and black pepper

Season the chicken with salt and pepper. Place a large, heavy-bottomed saucepan or frying pan with a lid over a medium heat and add the olive oil. When the oil is hot, add the garlic cloves and fry gently until slightly golden. Remove with a spoon and set aside. Now add the chicken, in batches, and fry for 3 minutes on either side until golden brown all over. Return the garlic to the pan along with the bay and pour in the wine, shaking the pan as you do so to help the wine emulsify with the oil. Simmer for 2 minutes to evaporate some alcohol, while turning the chicken in the sauce. Stir in the water, cover with a lid and simmer for 4 minutes. Take out any breast meat (if cooked), and put to one side. Continue to cook the brown meat for another 10 minutes. Add the breast back to the pot, season and add more water to the sauce if required. Taste for seasoning.

Chicken stuffed with garlic and coriander

The Moroccan flavours of coriander and cumin are mixed with sweet poached garlic and saffron, stuffed under the skin of a chicken and roasted. For this recipe, you can either bone the chicken as described on page 216 or roast it whole.

Serves 4

1 medium organic or free-range chicken, about 1.5 kg

olive oil

juice of ½ lemon (optional)

sea salt and black pepper

STUFFING

3 garlic bulbs

enough milk to cover the garlic in a small saucepan by at least 3cm

approx. 40 saffron threads (see page 172)

1 small bunch fresh coriander, roughly chopped

1½ level teaspoons ground cumin

3 teaspoons olive oil

For the stuffing, break up the garlic bulbs, discarding any woody roots and imperfect cloves, and simmer, skins on, in the milk for 25 minutes. When the garlic is soft, put your saffron in a cup to infuse with approximately 2–3 tablespoons of the hot garlic milk. Drain the rest of the milk away and put the garlic through a mouli or squeeze out the soft centre of each clove and mash to a purée. Now add the saffron and its milk, the coriander, cumin and olive oil and stir together. Season to taste with salt and pepper. With your hands, gently ease the skin of the chicken away from the breast and thigh to form a pocket either side. It is now ready to stuff. Place the garlic paste under the skin a teaspoon at a time until as much of the area is filled as possible. Try to get some stuffing in and around the thigh and drumstick. If you have any spare stuffing, simply put it inside the cavity of the chicken.

Preheat the oven to 220°C/425°F/Gas 7.

To cook the boned chicken, follow the instructions on page 216. For a whole chicken, season the chicken on the outside with a drop of olive oil, salt and pepper. Place in a lightly oiled roasting tin and put in the hot oven to roast for about an hour, basting every now and then. After about 50 minutes, test the leg with a skewer. If the juices run clear, the chicken is cooked; if they are still pink, it will require a little more time. Transfer the chicken to a board and leave to rest for 10 minutes, loosely covered in foil.

The delicious garlicky stuffing complements not only the chicken, but whatever vegetable you decide to serve with it. To make a simple lemony gravy, skim off most of the fat from the roasting tray, and pour 100ml water in with the lemon juice, salt and pepper. Put the roasting tray on a medium heat and when it has come to the boil, scrape off any caramelised juices from the bottom. Season and pour into a warm jug ready to serve.

Pato asado con membrillo
ROAST DUCK WITH MEMBRILLO

We always feel that savoury dishes cooked with fruit should have the warning 'approach with extreme caution' because, although sweet/savoury dishes can be sublime, it is a delicate balance to achieve.

Serves 4

   1 Barbary or Gressingham duck, about 2.25–2.75kg, with its giblets
   Moros y Cristianos (see page 235), to serve
   sea salt and black pepper

STOCK
   1 onion
   1 carrot
   2 bay leaves, preferably fresh
   2 cloves
   a few black peppercorns

MEMBRILLO (QUINCE) SAUCE
   200ml medium oloroso sherry (see Sherry Suppliers)
   200ml duck stock (see above)
   120g membrillo (quince paste, see Spanish Suppliers)

Dry the skin of the duck thoroughly with kitchen paper, inside and out, and prick all over with a fork to help release the fat during cooking. Cut off the wing tips for the stock. If possible, leave in a cool, dry place for a few hours to dry further, or uncovered in the fridge overnight.

Preheat the oven to 230°C/450°F/Gas 8.

Rub the duck with a dessertspoon of fine sea salt and lay on a rack in a roasting tray, breast-side down. Roast at a high temperature for 15 minutes, then turn over and roast for a further 15 minutes or until the skin is a light mahogany colour and beginning to crisp. Turn the oven down to 180°C/350°F/Gas 4, and cook for a further 1½ hours.

Meanwhile, make a stock from the giblets and wing tips of the duck, the stock ingredients and enough water to cover by 2cm. Strain and skim off any fat and reduce the stock for half an hour to 200ml.

When the duck is cooked, remove to a board and leave to rest, loosely covered with foil. Pour off 95 per cent of the duck fat from the roasting tray and pour any juice from the cavity of the duck into the tray. Put the roasting tray over a low to medium heat and add the sherry. Simmer for a few minutes to burn off the alcohol, then add the duck stock and membrillo. Melt the membrillo and reduce for another few minutes. Season.

Quarter the duck and serve with Moros y Cristianos and the warm membrillo sauce.

Breast of duck with pomegranate molasses

This is a quick dish. We cook the duck medium-rare to pink and serve it with Okra with Pomegranate Molasses (see page 244).

Serves 4

 4 duck breasts, skin on
 2 tablespoons olive oil
 2 tablespoons water
 2 tablespoons pomegranate molasses (see page 125)
 a pinch of ground cinnamon
 sea salt and black pepper

Preheat the oven to 220°C/425°F/Gas 7. Score the skin of the breasts in a criss-cross fashion, salt well and leave for 15 minutes.

When you are ready, place a large frying pan with a heat-resistant handle over a medium heat and add the olive oil. Place the duck breasts skin-side down and seal for a minute or so until lightly browned. Turn over to seal the flesh, then place in the oven for approximately 15 minutes until pink. Remove and let the duck breasts rest on a board, loosely covered with foil, for 5-10 minutes.

Put the frying pan on the hob over a medium heat, pouring off any excess oil, then add the water, pomegranate molasses and cinnamon. Reduce for a minute and season with salt and pepper. Slice each breast into three to four pieces at an angle, pour the sauce over, and serve with the okra, or anything else you fancy.

Faisán con canela y castañas
PHEASANT WITH CLOVES, CINNAMON AND CHESTNUTS

A delicious, autumnal stew when pheasant and chestnuts are in season.

Serves 4

    6 tablespoons olive oil

    200g panceta (cured pork belly), skin off, cut into 1cm strips

    1 medium onion, finely chopped

    1 medium carrot, finely chopped

    3 garlic cloves, thinly sliced

    4 bay leaves, preferably fresh

    1 cinnamon stick

    2 sprigs fresh thyme

    ½ teaspoon sweet smoked Spanish paprika (see page 111)

    4 cloves, roughly ground

    1 x 400g tin plum tomatoes, drained of juice, broken up

    2 medium pheasants, jointed, each breast and leg cut in half

    200ml white wine

    200g chestnuts, boiled, fresh or vacuum-packed, roughly chopped

    sea salt and black pepper

Set a large saucepan over a medium heat and add half the olive oil. When hot, add the panceta and fry for about 5 minutes until it begins to colour. Now add the onion, carrot, garlic, bay leaves and cinnamon and cook for another 5–10 minutes until the vegetables have begun to caramelise. Add the thyme, paprika and cloves and stir well for a minute, then add the tomatoes and cook for 5 minutes, stirring occasionally.

Meanwhile place a large frying pan over a medium to high heat and add the remaining oil. Add the seasoned pieces of pheasant, skin-side down. Seal until brown on all sides, then remove and set aside. Add the legs to the saucepan first, followed by the white wine and gently simmer over a low heat with the lid half on for about 30–40 minutes or until no longer tough. Then add the chestnuts and breasts to the pot and continue cooking until the breasts are tender, but not dry, about 10 minutes. Check for seasoning and let the stew rest for a few minutes. We serve this with Mashed Potato with Garlic (see page 231) or basmati rice steamed with a few coriander seeds, and watercress.

VEGETABLES

Our enthusiasm for vegetables never seems to diminish. The wonderful thing about them is that each one has many personas depending on how it is cooked, let alone what flavours it is seasoned with. For us, the secret is to be relatively strict about seasonal buying, so that vegetables – and fruit – are never taken for granted and always eaten at their best. As one season draws to an end, we always look forward to the next, with the different recipes and new ideas it brings with it. If you are reliant on supermarket vegetables this approach can be difficult to follow. Supermarkets tell us their customers want choice all year round, which in effect can mean a choice of uninspiring, tasteless fruit and vegetables. With a small greengrocer, on the other hand, it is possible to speak directly to the person who goes to the market, but it is up to you to know and ask them 'When do the first Sicilian tomatoes arrive?' Or 'When are the first English asparagus available?' At Moro, a vegetable's season will start being supplied by the warm Mediterranean and will finish two to three months later from organic farms in England. We support organic produce as much as possible, providing the variety and season is right, otherwise the flavour counts for nothing. For a general guide to seasonal vegetables and fruit, see the page 283.

The role of vegetables within the Moro menu is two-fold – as dishes in their own right and to complete meat and fish plates. The recipes in this chapter are just some of our vegetable recipes. Others may be found in the chapters on tapas and mezze (see page 21) and vegetable starters (see page 135), and all can be used to make up Moro plates, providing they are culturally and seasonally relevant.

Guisantes y patatas
PEAS AND POTATOES WITH ANIS

At Moro, for any recipes that involve peas, we try to use small, sweet fresh peas when they are in season, but we often find they get very large very quickly and lose all their flavour and tenderness. A good variety of frozen pea is one of those rare exceptions where something frozen can be a better standard than something fresh. In this Spanish dish, the flavour of aniseed goes well with the peas and is especially delicious with pork.

Serves 4

    4 tablespoons olive oil
    1 large Spanish onion, finely chopped
    2 garlic cloves, thinly sliced
    2 bay leaves, preferably fresh
    500g firm, waxy potatoes, such as Cyprus, peeled, quartered length-
        ways, chopped into small cubes and lightly salted
    1 medium carrot, finely diced
    150ml sweet anis liqueur
    500g podded peas, fresh or frozen
    1 small bunch fresh mint, roughly chopped
    sea salt and black pepper

In a large saucepan, heat the olive oil over a low to medium heat and add the onion with a pinch of salt. Cook for about 15–20 minutes, stirring occasionally, until the onion is golden and sweet. Now add the garlic, bay leaves, potatoes, carrot, salt and pepper and cook for 10 more minutes. Pour in the anis, simmer gently, and when the potatoes are almost tender, stir in the peas and mint. When the peas are cooked, about 5 minutes, check for seasoning and add a little water if the mixture becomes too dry.

Patatas a lo pobre
POOR MAN'S POTATOES

This dish may be simple, and called 'poor man's potatoes', but there is something about potatoes simmered in olive oil with garlic and peppers that is inexplicably good. Like other classic recipes, we have tasted different variations throughout Andalucía. They may come with red pepper instead of green, or without any pepper, but with chopped egg. This version is perfect with a piece of meat or fish, or on its own.

Serves 4

      15 tablespoons olive oil

      3 large Spanish onions, thinly sliced

      5 garlic cloves, thickly sliced

      3 green peppers, halved, seeded and roughly chopped

      4 bay leaves, preferably fresh

      1 kg firm, waxy potatoes, such as Cyprus, peeled

      sea salt and black pepper

Set a large saucepan over a medium heat and add 5 tablespoons of the olive oil. When the oil is hot, add the onion and a pinch of salt. Cook the onion slowly, turning down the heat if necessary, for about 20-30 minutes, stirring occasionally, until golden and sweet in smell and taste. Now add the garlic, pepper and bay and cook for 15 more minutes to release their flavour. Meanwhile, cut the potatoes in half lengthways and each half in two or three wedges, depending on the size of the potato. Salt them lightly and leave for about 5 minutes. When the pepper has softened, add the remaining oil and when the oil is hot again, add the potatoes. Let everything simmer gently, stirring occasionally, for another 15-20 minutes or until the potatoes are tender. Drain in a colander or sieve, keeping the onion oil aside for further use (like Caramelised Crispy Onions, see page 172). We serve patatas a lo pobre with roast pork or grilled lamb (see Meat Main Courses).

Mashed potato with garlic

The flavour of garlic in this mashed potato is by no means aggressive – it is subtle and sweet instead.

Serves 4

- 1 kg potatoes (Désirée, Wilja or Cyprus), peeled and cut in quarters
- 1 garlic bulb, cloves separated and peeled
- 2 bay leaves, preferably fresh
- 750ml milk
- 750ml water
- 3 tablespoons olive oil
- sea salt and black pepper

In a large saucepan, cover the potatoes, garlic and bay leaves with the milk and water. Set over a high heat, bring to the boil and reduce the heat to a gentle simmer. Cook for about 15 minutes or until the potatoes are soft. Drain in a colander and keep 200ml of the cooking liquid aside but discard the bay leaves. Mash the potatoes and garlic either by hand or through a mouli. Add some of the cooking liquid until it is the consistency that you like, stir in the olive oil and season with salt and pepper.

Patatas bravas

'Patatas bravas' are fried potatoes with a spicy tomato sauce, traditionally served as a tapa or as an accompanying vegetable for a main course such as grilled lamb. We like the sauce to be quite 'picante' (hot), probably more so than your average Spaniard, who is surprisingly sensitive to spicy food. We also start off cooking this sauce in two pans to reduce the cooking time.

Serves 4

FRIED POTATOES

1.5 kg potatoes (Cyprus or any firm, waxy potato), peeled, cubed and lightly salted

1 litre sunflower or olive oil, or a mixture of the two

sea salt, preferably Maldon

smoked Spanish paprika (see page 111)

BRAVAS SAUCE

2 x 400g tins plum tomatoes in their own juice

6 tablespoons olive oil

4 garlic cloves, thinly sliced

1-2 small dried red chillies, crumbled

2 bay leaves, preferably fresh

⅓ teaspoon each of dried thyme and oregano

1 large Spanish onion, finely chopped

1 green pepper, halved, seeded and finely chopped

100ml dry white wine

½ teaspoon caster sugar

1 teaspoon hot Spanish paprika (see Suppliers)

sea salt and black pepper

For the sauce, pour the tomatoes into a bowl and squash them well, removing any hard bits and skin. Pour half of the olive oil into a large saucepan over a medium heat and fry the garlic. When the garlic is golden, add the chilli and stir briefly. Now add the tomatoes and herbs and bring to a gentle simmer, turning down the heat if necessary. Cook for about 20 minutes until the tomato juice has more or less evaporated. Remove from the heat. Meanwhile, in another saucepan, sauté the chopped onion and pepper in the rest of the olive oil also for about 20 minutes until they become soft and sweet and caramelise slightly. Now add the white wine to the onion mixture, bring to the boil and pour in the tomatoes from the other saucepan. Stir in the sugar and paprika, and season with salt and pepper. Cook for 5 more minutes, adding some water if the sauce is too thick. Set aside.

Blanch the potatoes in the oil over a medium heat until tender without colouring. (This can be done in advance.) Then fry in hot but not smoking oil until golden brown. Drain, and taste for salt.

Spoon the warmed sauce over the potatoes and sprinkle with extra paprika. Sometimes in Spain, this dish is also served with mayonnaise or alioli.

Acelgas
BLANCHED CHARD, DRESSED OR BRAISED

Blanching, that is, boiling vegetables briefly in water, is a useful way of cooking chard, although you can, with equal success, blanch any number of vegetables such as spinach, asparagus, peas, green beans, sprouting broccoli, broad beans, cauliflower, beetroot tops and cabbage.

Serves 4

    1 kg chard, red, white or Swiss, stalks removed and kept separate
    sea salt and black pepper

Bring a large saucepan of salted water to a rolling or proper boil (the salt fixes the green colour in the vegetable, as well as bringing out the flavour). Add the leaves and put on the lid to ensure the water will come back to the boil as quickly as possible. When the leaves are tender, about 1–2 minutes, immediately scoop out and place in a colander and, if required, cool under running water. Now blanch the stalks, bearing in mind they will take longer.

DRESSED CHARD
    juice of ½ lemon
    2–3 tablespoons olive oil
    sea salt and black pepper

At this stage, you can dress the chard (and other vegetables), either hot or cold, with lemon juice, olive oil, salt and pepper. Chard needs gentle squeezing to get rid of excess water.

BRAISED CHARD
    4 tablespoons olive oil
    3–4 garlic cloves, thinly sliced
    sea salt and black pepper

Braising is a useful technique for flavouring vegetables with slices of garlic lightly fried in olive oil. Place a large saucepan over a medium heat, add the olive oil and when it is hot, the garlic. Gently fry until the garlic turns golden, then add your blanched chard, toss in the oil and season with salt and pepper. Remove from the heat immediately as it does not require any more cooking.

If you were braising spinach, it would not need blanching first as the leaves are tender enough.

Moros y Cristianos
MOORS AND CHRISTIANS (BLACK BEANS WITH RICE)

This recipe is another reminder of the Moors' place in Spanish history; a visual as well as culinary reference with the black beans and white rice. We like to serve Moros y Cristianos with roast duck (see page 222).

Serves 4

150g black beans (frijoles negros), soaked overnight

½ medium onion

2 garlic cloves

2 bay leaves, preferably fresh

½ cinnamon stick

zest of ½ orange

juice of ½ orange

3 tablespoons olive oil

½ small bunch fresh flat-leaf parsley, roughly chopped

150g white rice (like calasparra, see page 160)

sea salt and black pepper

Drain the beans and place in a large saucepan with at least six times their volume of cold water. Add the onion, garlic, bay leaves and cinnamon stick and cook according to the guidelines on page 113. Season with salt and pepper, the orange zest, orange juice, olive oil and parsley and set aside.

Simmer the rice in lightly salted boiling water until firm but not chalky (about 10–15 minutes), and drain. When you are ready, serve the rice, then spoon the beans and a little of their juices on top, so you can see both the white and the black.

Cauliflower with saffron, pinenuts and raisins

The white cauliflower shows off the saffron's colour beautifully and turns this parochial vegetable into quite a glamorous one.

Serves 4

  1 medium cauliflower, broken into small florets (keep the smallest
  leaves)

  3 tablespoons olive oil

  1 large Spanish onion, thinly sliced

  50 strands saffron, infused in 4 tablespoons boiling water

  3 tablespoons pinenuts, lightly toasted

  75g raisins, soaked in warm water

  sea salt and black pepper

Bring a large saucepan of salted water to the boil. Add the cauliflower, put the lid on and bring to the boil again. Blanch the cauliflower for a minute, then drain in a colander and set aside.

Heat the olive oil in a heavy saucepan until hot but not smoking then add the onion with a pinch of salt. Stir well, reduce the heat to low and cook very slowly for about 15-20 minutes until golden in colour and sweet in smell. Be sure to stir the onions every 5 minutes so they cook evenly and do not stick to the bottom of the pan. Remove from the heat, drain the onion and keep the oil.

Set the same saucepan over a high heat and add the olive oil back to the pan. When the oil is hot, add the cauliflower and leaves. Fry until the cauliflower begins to colour, then add the onion, the saffron-infused water, the pinenuts and drained raisins. Give everything a good toss and cook for 5 more minutes until the saffron water has more or less evaporated. Season with salt and pepper and serve.

Ensalada de espinaca y alcachofas de Jerusalen

SPINACH AND JERUSALEM ARTICHOKE SALAD

This is a colourful, crunchy salad for those who want to eat something light with a piece of meat or fish.

500g young spinach leaves, washed and dried
500g Jerusalem artichokes, peeled and sliced paper-thin
Sherry Vinegar Dressing (see page 258)

In a large salad bowl, toss the spinach, Jerusalem artichokes and dressing together until evenly mixed. Taste for seasoning. Jerusalem artichokes will discolour if not dressed immediately, so if you want to prepare things beforehand, immerse them in cold water until you are ready. This salad is delicious with grilled lamb and Romesco (see page 252).

Escalivada
GRILLED VEGETABLE SALAD

'Escalivada' originates from Catalunya in north-eastern Spain. It gets its
name from the Catalan 'escalivar' which means 'to char', for traditionally
the vegetables are cooked over hot coals. Nowadays a barbecue is ideal for
making escalivada as charcoal imparts that magical smoky flavour, which is
more difficult to achieve with conventional ovens. It is an amazingly versatile salad that can be served as a starter, with toast and salted anchovies, or
with most meat or fish. It can be served warm or at room temperature (so
may be prepared in advance) but never fridge cold. It is better to make this
salad in late spring or summer when the peppers, tomatoes and aubergines
are in season.

Serves 4

> 2 large whole red bell peppers
> 1 large Spanish onion
> 2 aubergines
> 4 sweet tomatoes
> olive oil
> Sherry Vinegar (or red wine vinegar) Dressing (see page 258)
> 1 small bunch fresh flat-leaf parsley, roughly chopped
> sea salt and black pepper

Preheat the oven to 190°C/375°F/Gas 5.

If you do not have a barbecue, first place the whole vegetables under a hot grill or on the naked flame of a gas hob until the skins are charred and crispy. Then place in the preheated oven in a lightly oiled roasting tin on the middle shelf. The length of time you cook the vegetables for is easy. Onions and tomatoes need extra time to sweeten and concentrate their flavours. Allow a good 1–1½ hours, whereas the aubergines and red peppers only need about 20 minutes, or until the flesh is soft.

Remove the vegetables and cool a little. Peel the charred skin off the peppers, aubergines and onions. Tear the flesh into large strips, the tomatoes in half, discarding the seeds, stalk and core of the peppers. Dress the vegetables with the dressing while still warm, add the chopped parsley, and season.

Green beans with cinnamon and yoghurt

This Lebanese recipe is perfect with chicken or fish. Choose new season's beans, for larger stringier varieties will ruin the dish.

Serves 4
  1 garlic clove, crushed to a paste with salt
  1 teaspoon ground cinnamon
  400g home-made or Greek yoghurt, thinned with 1 tablespoon milk
  700g young or fine green or French beans, tailed
  sea salt and black pepper

In a small mixing bowl, combine the garlic, cinnamon and yoghurt and check for seasoning. Fill a large saucepan with water and bring to the boil. When the water begins to boil, add the green beans and put the lid on. When the water comes back to the boil, simmer for 1–2 minutes then test a bean to see if it is tender. Place a colander in the sink, pour in the beans, discarding the water, and let the beans sit for a minute or two to drain off any excess water. Place the hot beans in a mixing bowl, pour on the seasoned yoghurt and toss well. Serve immediately. These beans are also delicious cold on a warm day.

Turlu Turlu

Turlu turlu, so good they named it twice, is Turkish in origin. It is like a spiced and exotically herbed ratatouille, although the roasting of the vegetables adds sweetness and complexity of texture. At Moro we serve turlu turlu as a vegetarian main course with rocket salad and yoghurt sauce, but it is also perfect with grilled meat or fish.

Serves 4

> 3 courgettes, trimmed and cut into 2cm discs
>
> 1 aubergine, halved lengthways and each ½ cut into 4 wedges lengthways
>
> 1 medium onion, roughly chopped
>
> 3 garlic cloves, thickly sliced
>
> 2 green peppers, halved, seeded and thickly sliced
>
> 3 medium carrots, peeled, halved lengthways and each ½ cut in 3 lengthways
>
> 200g turnips, cut into wedges about 2cm thick
>
> 2 medium potatoes, cut into 2cm cubes
>
> 3 tablespoons extra virgin olive oil
>
> ½ teaspoon ground allspice
>
> 2 teaspoons coriander seeds
>
> 3 tablespoons cooked chickpeas
>
> 150ml tomato passata or Sweet Tomato Sauce (see page 257)
>
> 1 small bunch each of fresh flat-leaf parsley and coriander, roughly chopped
>
> sea salt and black pepper

Preheat the oven to 220°C/425°F/Gas 7.

Sprinkle a teaspoon of fine sea salt on the courgettes and aubergine and let them stand for 20 minutes before rinsing under cold water.

In a large bowl toss the aubergine, onion, garlic, peppers, carrots, turnips and potatoes with the olive oil, allspice, coriander seeds and a little salt and pepper. Now spread out the vegetable mixture in a large roasting tray, no more than one layer deep (otherwise the vegetables steam rather than roast) and place in the preheated oven. The idea is that some of the vegetables colour or caramelise while roasting but are gently turned in the tray every 15 minutes to prevent burning. After 45 minutes, gently stir in the courgettes and cook for another 15 minutes.

Meanwhile heat up the chickpeas with the passata or tomato sauce in a pan, and check for seasoning. Now add to your vegetables, stir in well along with your prepared herbs, and serve.

Turnips with vinegar

Pickled turnips are often eaten as part of a mezze for their crunch and slight radish taste. This interesting and punchy dish can be served as a mezze, but goes well with lamb too. Turnips are generally neglected in this country, but if cooked quickly, they are delicious.

Serves 4

> 3 tablespoons olive oil
> 1 kg turnips (if baby, keep whole, trim and wash thoroughly; if the
>   size of a tangerine, peel and quarter)
> 3 garlic cloves, finely chopped
> 4 tablespoons good-quality red wine vinegar
> sea salt and black pepper

Heat the oil in a large saucepan over a medium heat and when hot, add the prepared turnips. Fry quickly, stirring occasionally until the turnips begin to colour on all sides. Add the garlic and fry for another minute, then add the vinegar, salt and pepper. Cook for 2–5 minutes until the turnips lose part of their crunch but are not soft. Remove and taste for seasoning. The turnips may need more salt than you think because of the acidity of the vinegar.

Courgettes with pinenuts
and raisins

Sometimes we serve this as part of a mezze plate or with grilled fish and yoghurt and dill sauce (see page 255). A Spanish variation on this theme – spinach braised with pinenuts and raisins (often served with salted anchovies on top) – is a traditional dish from Seville, delicious on its own or with chicken or fish.

Serves 4

    1 kg small to medium courgettes, washed and both ends trimmed

    3–4 tablespoons olive oil

    1 large Spanish onion, thinly sliced

    75g raisins, soaked in warm water

    3 tablespoons pinenuts, lightly toasted

    sea salt and black pepper

Cut the courgettes in quarters or sixths lengthways depending on the size. If they are too long, cut them in half. If the seeds are spongy in texture, remove with a knife. Place in a colander over a sink or bowl, lightly salt and leave for about 20 minutes.

Meanwhile, heat the olive oil in a large saucepan and when it is hot but not smoking add the onion with a pinch of salt. Give it a good stir, reduce the heat to low and cook very slowly for about 20–30 minutes until golden in colour and sweet in smell. Be sure to stir the onions every 5 minutes so they cook evenly and do not stick to the bottom of the pan. Remove from the heat, drain the onion and keep the oil.

Give the courgettes a little wash to remove any excess salt and dry them with a cloth. Set the same saucepan over a high heat and return the olive oil to the pan. When the oil is hot, add the courgettes and cook for about 5 minutes, stirring every now and then until tender but not mushy. Drain the raisins and add to the courgettes along with the pinenuts and sweet onion. Taste for seasoning (they may only need a little pepper as the courgettes will be salty enough).

Okra with pomegranate molasses

Try to pick out the smallest okra you can find. Sometimes we use tiny frozen okra no more than 3cm long from Egypt or Lebanon, which you can buy in Lebanese or Iranian shops.

Serves 4

> 3 tablespoons olive oil
> 1 garlic clove, thinly sliced
> 1 kg small okra, ends trimmed and cut into 3cm pieces
> ½ teaspoon ground cinnamon
> 2 tablespoons pomegranate molasses (see page 125)
> 1 tablespoon water
> 1 small bunch fresh coriander, roughly chopped
> sea salt and black pepper

In a large saucepan or frying pan heat the olive oil over a medium heat. Fry the garlic until it begins to colour, then add the okra and a pinch of salt. Cook for 5 minutes, stirring occasionally, then add the cinnamon, pomegranate molasses, water and coriander and warm through. Season well.

Pinto beans with dill

This is a Turkish mezze dish, made with all sorts of beans. We use pinto beans or borlotti beans, especially when we can get them fresh from Italy and France during June and July. However you can use dried beans.

Serves 4

> 200g dried pinto or borlotti beans, or 500g fresh podded weight
>   (1.5 kg in pod)
> a few parsley, thyme or sage leaves and stalks
> ½ garlic bulb
> ½ small onion
> 1 tomato, pierced

1 small bunch fresh dill, roughly chopped
½ garlic clove, crushed to a paste with salt
3 tablespoons olive oil
sea salt and black pepper

If using dried beans, soak them for 12–24 hours. Rinse the beans and place in a large saucepan. Fill with cold water at least six times the volume of the beans, add the parsley, sage or thyme, garlic, onion and tomato and set over a high heat. When the water comes to the boil, reduce to a gentle simmer and cook for 1–2 hours or until the beans are cooked, depending a lot on whether they are fresh or dried. The skin should be soft and supple and the flesh creamy and smooth and in no way dry or have any bite to the flesh. Remember to skim any scum off the beans as it builds up.

When they are cooked, remove from the heat and pour off some of the cooking liquid until it is more or less level with the beans. Add the dill, crushed garlic and olive oil, and season to taste. This dish is delicious with lamb or fish or as a vegetable dish with globe artichokes and roast tomatoes.

Chickpea salad

This spicy, fresh salad is great as part of a mezze or with meat or fish. We serve it with Cod Baked with Tahini Sauce and Saffron Rice (see pages 187 and 170).

Serves 4

- 150g chickpeas, soaked overnight with a pinch of bicarbonate of soda, or 2 x 400g tins cooked chickpeas, rinsed
- 1 garlic clove, crushed to a paste with salt
- 1 large green chilli, halved lengthways, seeded and very finely diced
- ½ red onion, finely diced
- a squeeze of lemon
- 1 tablespoon red wine vinegar
- 4 tablespoons olive oil
- 1 medium cucumber, peeled and finely diced
- 10 cherry tomatoes, halved, seeded and finely diced
- 1 small bunch each of fresh mint and coriander, roughly chopped
- sea salt and black pepper

To cook the dried chickpeas, follow the instructions on page 138.

Put the garlic, chilli, onion, lemon juice, vinegar, olive oil, salt and pepper into a small mixing bowl. Stir well and then add the rest of the ingredients – the chickpeas, cucumber, tomatoes, mint and coriander. Taste for seasoning. Chill for a fresher taste.

SAUCES AND DRESSINGS

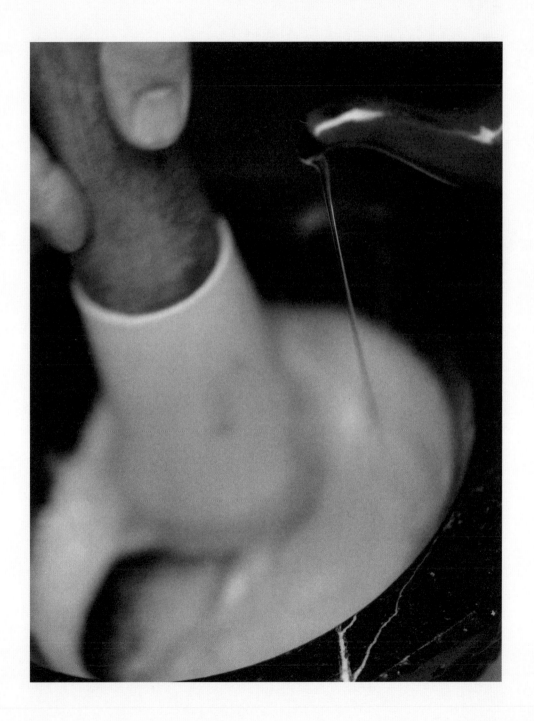

SAUCES

We use the heading 'sauces' in its loosest sense, for many of these recipes are closer to salsas or dressings. Whether they are made from pounded nuts, seasoned yoghurt or herbs, what they all have in common is that they are there to complement and enliven the food they are served with. Most are simple in technique, yet complex in flavour; they are also versatile enough to accompany different dishes as we have suggested throughout.

Alioli

The most famous of the Spanish garlic sauces is alioli. 'Alioli' literally means garlic and oil ('al-i-oli'), and is the garlic version of mayonnaise ('mahonesa' in Spanish), that was supposed to have originated from Mahón on the island of Menorca. Alioli is most satisfying made in a mortar and pestle, if your stirring arm is strong enough and your patience complete. Equally successfully it can be beaten in a mixing bowl with a balloon whisk, or in a food processor, although with this last method, care must be taken not to overwork the mixture, as this will cause it to split. This way is better suited to making larger quantities. If you must make alioli in a food processor, use a whole egg as well as an egg yolk. Though this makes a poorer cousin of pure egg yolk alioli in colour and texture, it is more stable. Proper alioli has lots of garlic, but this is up to your taste.

Serves 4

> 2-4 garlic cloves
> Maldon sea salt
> a good squeeze of lemon
> 2 egg yolks, organic or free-range
> 200ml oil (half extra virgin olive and half sunflower)

Crush the garlic cloves in a mortar and pestle with a pinch of salt. When smooth add the lemon juice. At this point you can transfer the garlic and egg yolks to a mixing bowl and whisk in the oil drop by drop with a balloon whisk. Otherwise continue in the mortar and pestle. Add the egg yolks and stir to break the membrane. Continue stirring, whilst you add the oil, painstakingly slowly at first, that is, drop by drop, then with more confidence when you see that a thick emulsion has formed. When all the oil is incorporated, season to taste with more salt and lemon juice if necessary. Serve with fish or grilled meat, rice dishes or vegetables.

CATALAN ALIOLI

Catalan alioli is a literal method for alioli, still practised today in Catalunya. A large amount of garlic (at least 8 cloves) is pounded with a few drops of water, followed by the oil. When the paste begins to thicken, add a few drops of vinegar and then the rest of the oil until a thick emulsion is formed. As you can imagine from the amount of garlic, it is extremely potent!

Quince alioli

A fruity version of alioli that goes well with pork and lamb especially. Made from membrillo, the quince paste, there is no need for egg to emulsify the sauce as the membrillo is thick enough. In fact, unlike normal alioli, it is difficult to split this, which is reassuring.

Serves 4
>250g membrillo (quince paste, see Spanish Suppliers and page 34)
>1 garlic clove
>150ml oil (half extra virgin olive and half sunflower)
>lemon juice to taste
>sea salt and black pepper

The method for making quince alioli is similar to the first alioli recipe, except that it is preferable to use a food processor or mixing bowl owing to the density of the membrillo. If you are using a mortar and pestle, melt the membrillo down first with a tiny bit of water over a low flame. This makes it easier to incorporate the oil. Crush the garlic with a little salt in a mortar and pestle. Transfer to a food processor, and add the membrillo. Blend, and slowly add the oil in a thin stream, resting occasionally, until all the oil is incorporated. Add more salt, pepper and lemon juice to taste.

Poached garlic sauce

We ate this sauce alongside a delicious steak in Bilbao, and back at Moro we have had equal success serving it with lamb. For this recipe a great deal of garlic is poached in milk, which gives the garlic a sweet, mellow and fragrant quality which is rather unusual.

Serves 4

    3 garlic bulbs
    enough milk to cover the garlic in a small saucepan by at least 3cm
    3 teaspoons extra virgin olive oil
    ½–¾ tablespoon sherry vinegar
    sea salt and black pepper

Break up the bulbs of garlic, discarding any woody roots, and simmer, skins on, in the milk for about 20 minutes or until the flesh inside is soft. Drain the rest of the milk away bar 6 tablespoons and put the garlic through a mouli or squeeze out the soft centre of each clove and mash to a purée. Add the reserved milk to thin it slightly, then stir in the olive oil and sherry vinegar. Season with salt and pepper.

Piquillo pepper sauce

We serve piquillo pepper sauce with asparagus, but it is also good with grilled lamb or fish. It can be made with or without salted anchovies.

Serves 4

    1 garlic clove
    1 teaspoon fresh thyme leaves
    3 salted anchovy fillets (optional)
    1 x 390g tin piquillo peppers (see page 27)
    1½ tablespoons good-quality red wine vinegar
    4 tablespoons extra virgin olive oil
    sea salt and black pepper

In a mortar and pestle, crush the garlic and thyme with a good pinch of salt until a greenish paste is formed. If you are using anchovy fillets, pound in with the garlic until smooth. Place the piquillo peppers in a food processor with their juice and pulse until totally smooth. Now add the garlic, anchovies (if using), vinegar and olive oil, and season with salt and pepper to taste.

Almond and sherry vinegar sauce

This sauce goes well with fish or chicken. See also the recipe for Cecina with Beetroot and Almond Sauce (page 121). When we serve this sauce with fish, we sometimes add capers.

Serves 4

> 150g whole blanched almonds
> 8–10 tablespoons water
> 25g stale white bread, crusts removed, soaked in water
> 1 garlic clove, crushed to a paste with salt
> 1 tablespoon extra virgin olive oil
> 1½ tablespoons capers soaked in water, squeezed and
>   finely chopped (optional)
> ½–¾ tablespoon sherry vinegar
> sea salt

In a food processor, grind the almonds until the consistency is as fine as possible. Now add 3 tablespoons of the water and process until the almonds form a paste. Squeeze the bread of excess water and add to the almonds along with the garlic. Combine until smooth. Slowly add the rest of the water and the olive oil, until you end up with a thick but smooth consistency similar to mayonnaise. Transfer to a bowl, add the capers if you are using them and season with sherry vinegar and salt to taste.

Romesco

Romesco is the famous Catalan sauce made with pounded almonds, hazelnuts and dried peppers. It is traditionally served in the province of Tarragona at the beginning of the year when 'calçots' (green onions) come into season. This occasion is often celebrated with a 'calçotada', a feast of calçots grilled over charcoal, then dipped in large bowls of romesco. Romesco is also wonderful with fish, chicken, lamb or grilled baby leeks and asparagus.

Serves 4

  - 100g whole blanched almonds
  - 50g shelled hazelnuts
  - 4 dried ñoras peppers (see page 163)
  - ½ dried guindilla pepper (see page 163), or 1 small dried red chilli, crumbled
  - 3 garlic cloves, peeled
  - 6 tablespoons olive oil
  - 50g stale white bread, cut into 1.5cm cubes
  - 150g piquillo peppers (see Spanish Suppliers), or 2 medium red bell peppers,
    roasted, peeled and seeded
  - 1–1½ tablespoons red wine vinegar or sherry vinegar, or a mixture of the two
  - 1 teaspoon tomato purée
  - 40 strands saffron, infused in 8 tablespoons boiling water (see page 172)
  - ½ teaspoon sweet smoked Spanish paprika (see page 111)
  - sea salt and black pepper

Preheat the oven to 180°C/350°F/Gas 4. Place the almonds and hazelnuts on a baking tray and dry-roast in the top of the oven for about 20 minutes or until light golden brown. Remove and cool. Meanwhile, break open the dried peppers and discard their seeds. Crumble the peppers a little further in a small bowl and cover with boiling water. Fry two of the garlic cloves whole in the olive oil until light brown. Remove the garlic with a slotted spoon and reserve. Now fry the cubes of bread in the same oil until they are also light brown. Keep the oil aside.

Traditionally, this sauce is made by pounding the bread, nuts, garlic and peppers (soaked and piquillo, keeping the pepper water aside) together in a mortar and pestle. If you do not have one, you may use a food processor. Once you have a coarse paste, transfer to a mixing bowl and stir in the olive oil, half the pepper water, the vinegar, the remaining garlic clove, crushed, the tomato purée, saffron, paprika, salt and pepper. Taste for seasoning. If the sauce is very thick, add a little water and/or more olive oil. Romesco can be made a few hours in advance, or the day before.

Fennel seed and parsley sauce

This sauce is a good accompaniment to pork or grilled fish. We prefer to make it in a mortar and pestle.

Serves 4

      1–2 garlic cloves

      5 tablespoons roughly chopped fresh flat-leaf parsley

      1½ teaspoons fennel seeds, ground

      4 tablespoons extra virgin olive oil

      juice of ½ lemon

      sea salt and black pepper

Crush the garlic with a good pinch of salt in a mortar and pestle until a smooth paste is formed. Now add the parsley to the mortar, a tablespoon at a time, and continue to pound until the parsley has become part of the paste. Add the fennel seeds and olive oil and stir well before adding the lemon juice. Always add the lemon juice after the oil, otherwise it will discolour the parsley. Season with salt and pepper.

Harissa

It is worth making your own harissa as some commercial pastes tend to be fiery but a little bitter and one-dimensional. With home-made harissa, you can really taste the spices and the chillies, and as it lasts well in the fridge, you can make enough to last for a couple of weeks. Harissa is traditionally served with couscous, eggs or bread, but gives zip to any dish. At Moro we also put it with grilled squid or brik.

Serves 6-8

>   250g long fresh red chillies
>   3 heaped teaspoons coarsely ground caraway seeds
>   3 heaped teaspoons coarsely ground cumin seeds
>   1 level teaspoon ground black cumin seeds (optional)
>   4 garlic cloves
>   100g piquillo peppers, or 1 large red bell pepper, roasted, peeled and
>   seeded
>   1 dessertspoon tomato purée
>   1 dessertspoon red wine vinegar
>   2 level teaspoons sweet smoked Spanish paprika (see page 111)
>   6 tablespoons extra virgin olive oil
>   sea salt and black pepper

It is advisable to wear rubber gloves when preparing the chillies. Slice the chillies in half lengthways. Lay each chilli on a chopping board cut-side up, gently scrape away the seeds with a teaspoon and discard them. Roughly chop the chillies and transfer to a food processor with a sharp blade. Blend the chillies with a pinch of salt, half of each of the spices and the garlic cloves until smooth. Then add the peppers and blend. It is important that the paste is as smooth as possible. Transfer to a mixing bowl. Now add the remaining ingredients – the rest of the spices, the peppers, tomato purée, vinegar, paprika and olive oil. Taste and season with more salt to balance out the vinegar. Harissa keeps well in the fridge, but be sure to cover it with a little olive oil to seal it from the air.

Yoghurt and pomegranate sauce

When pomegranates are in season at the end of the year, this jewel-like sauce makes anything look ravishing, fish and lamb especially. Another yoghurt sauce – also ideal with fish – is made with 200g yoghurt, chopped dill, garlic and seasoning.

Serves 4

> 150g home-made or Greek yoghurt, thinned with 1½ tablespoons milk
> ¼ garlic clove, crushed to a paste with salt
> seeds of 2 pomegranates, without the bitter yellow membrane
> 2 small bunches fresh flat-leaf parsley, roughly chopped
> sea salt and black pepper

In a mixing bowl, mix the yoghurt with the garlic, then stir in the pomegranate seeds and parsley and taste for seasoning.

Tahini sauce

Tahini paste is made from pounded sesame seeds, and is used throughout the Middle East in a variety of ways, delicious with fish or vegetables.

Serves 4

> 2 garlic cloves
> 3 tablespoons tahini paste (see page 186)
> juice of 1 lemon
> 5 tablespoons water
> sea salt and black pepper

Crush the garlic cloves to a paste with a good pinch of salt in a mortar and pestle. Transfer to a small mixing bowl. Whisk in the tahini and then thin with the lemon juice. Add water until you have a consistency of double cream. Check the seasoning.

Tarator

Tarator is a classic Turkish garlicky nut sauce eaten with vegetables, grilled fish or chicken. It is made with either walnuts, almonds, pinenuts or hazelnuts. We find the flavour of raw garlic goes particularly well with walnuts. Recently we have taken to tossing warm green beans as well as cucumber salad in this sauce.

Serves 4

>   150g shelled walnuts, soaked in boiling water for 1 hour to remove
>   any bitterness from the skins
>   30g stale white bread, crusts removed, soaked in water, then
>   squeezed
>   2 garlic cloves, crushed to a paste with salt
>   2–3 dessertspoons red wine vinegar
>   a good pinch of ground allspice
>   juice of ¼ lemon
>   6–10 tablespoons water
>   3 tablespoons extra virgin olive oil
>   sea salt and black pepper

Rinse and drain the walnuts, put in a food processor with the squeezed bread and blend well. This is slightly a matter of taste. The finer the nuts are chopped, the more mayonnaise-like the end result is. Combine the other ingredients and stir in. Season with salt and pepper. Roughly chopped fresh flat-leaf parsley or dill is a nice addition to this sauce.

Pistachio sauce

This emerald sauce usually goes with Quail Baked in Flatbread (see page 126), but it is also delicious with grilled lamb, chicken or white fish.

Serves 4

> 150g shelled unsalted pistachio nuts
>
> grated zest and juice of ½ lemon
>
> 1 tablespoon orange-blossom water (see page 274)
>
> 1 garlic clove, crushed to a paste with a little salt
>
> 1 small bunch fresh flat-leaf parsley, roughly chopped
>
> a few fresh mint leaves, roughly chopped
>
> 1 tablespoon water
>
> 5 tablespoons extra virgin olive oil
>
> sea salt and black pepper

In a mortar and pestle or food processor or by hand, roughly crush, blend or chop the nuts. Transfer to a mixing bowl, add the remaining ingredients and check for seasoning.

Sweet tomato sauce

This sauce is delicious even when made with tinned tomatoes. The secret is to caramelise the garlic in the olive oil and to cook the tomatoes slowly until they concentrate their flavour and become sweet. Sometimes we add a little spice at the same time as the garlic, such as cinnamon or chilli when the recipe calls for it.

Serves 4

> 2 x 400g tins whole plum tomatoes, drained of juice,
>
> or 1 kg sweet fresh tomatoes
>
> 4 tablespoons olive oil
>
> 6 garlic cloves, thinly sliced
>
> sea salt and black pepper

If you are using fresh tomatoes, you need to blanch them to loosen the skins. To do this, break off the stalk, make a little slit in each skin and pour over enough boiling water to cover them. Count to twenty and refresh with cold water until they are easy to handle. Remove the skins and discard. Cut the tomatoes in half across, seed them and remove any hard core. With the tinned tomatoes, place in a bowl and mash up with your hands, throwing away any bits of skin or core.

In a medium-sized saucepan, heat the olive oil over a medium to high heat. When the oil is hot, but not smoking, add the garlic and fry until the garlic begins to colour. Add the chopped tomatoes and a pinch of salt to balance their acidity. Cook over a medium heat until most of the liquid that the tomatoes give out has evaporated. Taste for seasoning.

DRESSINGS

As a rule we make dressings with vinegar (usually sherry vinegar and red wine vinegar) when the recipe is Spanish, while the dressings for our Muslim Mediterranean dishes are generally made with lemon juice.

Sherry vinegar dressing

Sherry vinegar gives salad dressing an unusual, nutty and complex flavour. Try to get hold of an aged sherry vinegar whenever possible as it is less astringent and has more character. Valdespino is a good make (see page 194). Sherry vinegar may be substituted by a good red wine vinegar.

Serves 4

    1 garlic clove

    1 tablespoon sherry vinegar (or red wine vinegar)

    a squeeze of lemon (optional)

    4 tablespoons extra virgin olive oil

    sea salt and black pepper

Crush the garlic with a good pinch of salt in a mortar and pestle until a smooth paste is formed. Then add the vinegar and lemon juice (if using), and whisk in the olive oil. Season with salt and pepper. This can be made a few hours earlier, but not the day before because the garlic will taste stale. Give it a good whisk just before using.

Pedro Ximénez dressing

Miguel Valdespino from the famous sherry bodega gave this recipe to us. The dressing is made by mixing equal quantities of sherry vinegar and Pedro Ximénez sherry (the sweet, raisiny sherry). What you end up with is a dressing that has all the nutty complexity of the sherry vinegar dressing, but with a slightly sweeter, raisiny finish. This is delicious with a chicory salad with blue cheese, parsley and walnuts such as we make in the restaurant, but is compatible with many other things, such as tomato salad.

Serves 4

   1 garlic clove
   ½ tablespoon sherry vinegar
   ½ tablespoon Pedro Ximénez sherry (see Sherry Suppliers)
   a squeeze of lemon (optional)
   4 tablespoons extra virgin olive oil
   sea salt and black pepper

Crush the garlic with a good pinch of salt in a mortar and pestle until a smooth paste is formed. Then add the vinegar, sherry and lemon juice (if using), and whisk in the olive oil until emulsified. Season with salt and pepper. This can be made a few hours earlier, but not the day before because the garlic will taste a little stale. Give it a good whisk just before using.

Lemon dressing

A light lemon dressing with or without garlic that we use for our Muslim Mediterranean recipes and Spanish recipes when the flavour of sherry vinegar is too distinctive and we want a change from red wine vinegar.

Serves 4

      1 garlic clove (optional)
      1½ tablespoons lemon juice
      4 tablespoons extra virgin olive oil
      sea salt and black pepper

Crush the garlic (if using) with a good pinch of salt in a mortar and pestle until a smooth paste is formed. Then add the lemon juice and whisk in the olive oil. Season with salt and pepper. This can be made a few hours earlier, but give it a good whisk just before using.

Pomegranate molasses dressing

This exotic dressing is made from concentrated pomegranate juice. It goes well not only with salad but also with braised spinach, quail or fish.

Serves 4

      1 garlic clove, crushed to a paste with salt
      ¼ teaspoon ground cinnamon
      2 tablespoons pomegranate molasses (see page 125)
      1 tablespoon water
      4 tablespoons extra virgin olive oil
      ½ teaspoon caster sugar (optional)
      sea salt and black pepper

Mix the garlic with the cinnamon and pomegranate molasses, then add the water and whisk in the olive oil. The sauce should emulsify. Check for seasoning, adding sugar if the dressing is very tart.

PUDDINGS

We are very proud of our puddings at Moro. Unlike other recipes in the book, these puddings are inspired by flavours and ingredients rather than being classic dishes from a specific country. We combine these ingredients with techniques we have learnt along the way such as the use of apricot paste in a rich chocolate tart or membrillo (quince paste) in the Santiago tart, and as a result, they have become Moro classics in their own right. Where appropriate we serve these puddings with thick, creamy yoghurt that we make ourselves in the restaurant (see page 50) to balance out the sweetness, but you may also use crème fraîche.

Sweet pastry tart shell

This pastry will fill a 24cm tart tin with a loose bottom, and will serve six. The raw dough can be made in advance and chilled, or frozen.

Makes approx. 250g pastry

> 140g plain flour
> 30g icing sugar
> 75g chilled butter, cut into small pieces
> 1 egg yolk

Sift the flour and icing sugar together. In a food processor or by hand, blend the butter with the flour until you have a texture similar to fine breadcrumbs. Add the egg yolk and mix until the ingredients more or less come together. If the pastry looks too dry add a tiny splash of milk or water. Shape into a ball, flatten slightly, wrap in clingfilm and chill in the fridge for a minimum of an hour.

When you are ready, grate the pastry (it can be quite hard) on a coarse grater and press it evenly around the edges and base of the tart tin to a thickness of 3-5mm. Prick the base and rest in the fridge for 30 minutes. Meanwhile, preheat the oven to 220°C/425°F/Gas 7. Bake the tart shell in the top shelf of the oven for 10-15 minutes until light brown. Remove and cool on a rack.

Tarta de cerezas
CHERRY AND CUSTARD TART

Poaching cherries in anis (a Spanish liqueur made from aniseed) can make even the dullest cherries delicious. If you have neither time nor energy to make the pastry, the cherries eaten with custard are very good.

Serves 6

1 x Sweet Pastry Tart Shell (see opposite)

CHERRIES AND SYRUP
500g cherries, washed, drained and stalks removed
about 400ml sweet anis to cover
2 tablespoons caster sugar
juice of ½ lemon

CUSTARD
300ml milk
300ml double cream
rind of ⅔ lemon, in large thin strips without the pith
½ vanilla pod, split in half lengthways
4 egg yolks
2 eggs
30g caster sugar

Follow the instructions opposite for cooking the pastry shell, then remove to a rack.

Place the cherries and anis in a saucepan over a medium heat and put the lid on. Cook for about 5 minutes until the cherries start to lose their juice, but keep their firmness and shape. Remove, drain and keep the juice. Stone the cherries, adding any juice from that to the other juice. To make the syrup, boil the juice for 5 minutes on a high heat with the sugar, then add the lemon juice to taste. The syrup should be the tiniest bit sharp. Cool down and set aside.

To make the custard, place the milk, cream and lemon rind in a saucepan. Scrape the seeds from the vanilla pod and add to the pan along with the pod. Simmer everything gently for 5 minutes. Remove from the heat and whisk in the egg yolks, eggs and sugar. Now cook over a very low heat, stirring constantly in the same direction for 15–20 minutes, until thick. Remove the pan from the heat, pour the custard into a bowl (strain if necessary) and place over iced water to cool. If the custard goes lumpy while you are cooking it, place the pan in iced water and whisk well.

When you are ready to assemble your tart, preheat the oven to 180°C/350°F/Gas 4.

Place the cherries on the tart shell in circles starting around the edge and working in, leaving a little gap in between. Next pour the custard on top of the cherries. Bake the tart on the top shelf of the preheated oven until the custard sets, about 20 minutes. The custard should feel firm but still wobbly. Remove the tart, cool on a rack and serve with the cherry syrup on the side.

Tarta de Santiago
ALMOND TART WITH OLOROSO

This tart from Galicia is traditionally served in Santiago on St James's Day. We have added membrillo, to create something rather like a Spanish version of Bakewell tart, which goes well with the almonds and oloroso sherry.

Serves 6

1 x Sweet Pastry Tart Shell (see page 262)

FILLING

130g membrillo (quince paste, see Spanish Suppliers and page 34)

1 tablespoon water

1 tablespoon lemon juice

230g blanched almonds, ¼ processed to chunky, the rest medium

finely grated zest of ¾ orange and ¾ lemon

1½ small cinnamon sticks, finely ground

40ml oloroso sherry (see Sherry Suppliers)

115g unsalted butter, softened

75g caster sugar

2 eggs

Follow the instructions on page 262 for cooking the pastry shell, then remove to a rack. Preheat the oven to 180°C/350°F/Gas 4.

In a pan melt the membrillo with the water and lemon juice over a low heat so it does not stick. Stir out the lumps and spread evenly on the bottom of the cooled tart shell. Set aside. Mix the almonds, orange and lemon zests, cinnamon and sherry and leave for 5 minutes for the flavours to mingle. Meanwhile, beat the butter and sugar together until pale, soft and fluffy, then add the eggs one by one. The mixture will look lumpy and not emulsified. Now fold the almond mixture into the eggs, ease into the pastry shell and spread out roughly.

Bake the tart on the middle shelf of the preheated oven for about 30–40 minutes until a golden brown crust has formed. Serve with yoghurt or crème fraîche.

Torta de naranja
ORANGE AND ALMOND TORTA

Oranges, almonds and cinnamon are all Moorish ingredients that remind us so much of southern Spain and which are the main ingredients of this equally Moorish cake. We sometimes use Seville oranges instead of normal oranges when they are in season for a slightly tarter finish.

Serves 6

    6 eggs, separated
    240g caster sugar
    230g almonds, almost finely ground
    finely grated zest of 2½ oranges

    SYRUP
    juice of 8 oranges or 8 Seville oranges
    juice of 1½ lemons (if not using Seville oranges)
    1 whole cinnamon stick
    caster sugar to taste

Preheat the oven to 180°C/350°F/Gas 4. Line a 23cm spring-form tin on the bottom and sides with greaseproof paper.

Keeping 1 tablespoon of caster sugar aside for later, mix the egg yolks and sugar together until pale. Then add the almonds and zest. Beat the egg whites and remaining tablespoon of sugar until stiff and carefully fold into the sugar-egg mixture, trying not to knock the air out of the whites. The egg yolk/sugar mixture will seem very stiff at first, but keep folding in the egg whites and it will soon loosen up. Gently ease into the lined tin, place on the middle shelf of the oven, and bake for about 60–70 minutes until the torta is golden on top and firm to the touch.

While the torta is in the oven, make the syrup. Place the orange juice, lemon juice and cinnamon stick in a saucepan with a handful of sugar, bring to a gentle boil and simmer for about 5 minutes. Taste. The syrup should be quite tart. Allow to cool and place in the fridge.

When the torta is ready, remove from the oven and cool completely on a rack before opening the spring-form tin. Transfer to a plate and with a skewer, pierce four small holes in the top of the cake and pour half the syrup over the top. Serve with the rest of the syrup on the side.

Tarta de naranjas sevillanas
SEVILLE ORANGE TART

Seville oranges appear in English markets in December/early January, primarily to make marmalade. We use them to make a sharp orange curd that we pour into a pastry shell and serve with creamy yoghurt or crème fraîche.

Serves 6

1 x Sweet Pastry Tart Shell (see page 262)

SEVILLE ORANGE CURD
140g caster sugar
170ml Seville orange juice
170g unsalted butter, cut into small pieces
4 egg yolks, organic or free-range
2 eggs
finely grated zest of ¼ orange

Follow the instructions on page 262 for cooking the pastry shell, then remove to a rack.

Mix all the curd ingredients together and cook very slowly, stirring constantly, for 15–20 minutes until thick. To start off with, the mixture will not seem to thicken – this will happen suddenly at the end - so do not be tempted to turn the heat up or it will curdle. Remove when the custard is thick, but still a pourable consistency.

Meanwhile preheat the oven to 240°C/475°F/Gas 9. Spread the curd into the tart shell and bake for 10 minutes on the top shelf of the preheated oven until it starts to colour, making sure it does not split. Cool on a rack before serving.

Churros con chocolate

Every town in Spain has at least one 'churreria', where you can buy lines or coils of fried doughnuts to dip in thick, rich hot chocolate or 'cafe con leche' (milky coffee) for breakfast. Churros are one of those Spanish institutions, popular with all ages and a great opportunity for chatting with friends and family or people-watching. At Moro we serve churros as a pudding, with a glass of chilled chocolate.

Serves 6

CHURROS

400g plain flour

a pinch of salt

1 teaspoon bicarbonate of soda

400ml boiling water

750ml sunflower oil for deep-frying

caster sugar for dusting

CHOCOLATE

1 small cinnamon stick

400ml milk

300g dark chocolate (like Valrhona, 70% cocoa solids), broken up

250ml sweetened condensed milk

250ml double cream

To make the churros batter, sift the flour and salt into a large mixing bowl and make a well in the centre. Pour in the water, then with a balloon whisk gently mix in, stirring all the while so no lumps form. When all the water is incorporated, beat well until smooth. Transfer to a saucepan and cook over a low heat, stirring constantly, for 1-2 minutes. Remove from the heat, spoon the mixture into a bowl and leave to rest for an hour.

To make the chocolate, infuse the cinnamon in the milk by simmering it for 15 minutes. Remove from the heat and discard the cinnamon. Meanwhile, melt the chocolate in a bain-marie. When melted, gently stir in the infused milk and condensed milk until smooth and emulsified. Pour into six tumblers. Whisk the cream until soft peaks form and spoon on top of the chocolate. Chill in the fridge for at least an hour.

To cook the churros, heat the oil in a large saucepan over a medium heat until hot. Meanwhile, transfer the batter to a churros maker or piping bag with a small nozzle. Squeeze the batter into the hot oil to form a line or coil, and fry until golden brown. Make sure the oil is not too hot, otherwise the churros will colour too much before cooking through; neither should it be too cool, otherwise the churros will disintegrate. Remove and drain on kitchen paper. Dust liberally with sugar and serve immediately with the chocolate.

Fresas en Moscatel con mantecados

STRAWBERRIES IN MOSCATEL WITH SANDCAKES

Along the Alameda Principal in Málaga, there is a bar called Antigua Casa de Guardia that has been open for 150 years. It is lined with huge old casks filled with a wonderful selection of Málaga wines. One of these is Moscatel, a sweet but complex wine made from the Moscatel grape. We marinate strawberries in this amber nectar, and serve them with 'mantecados', Moorish cinnamon sandcakes.

Serves 8

> 800g strawberries, washed, drained and stalks removed
> 560ml Moscatel Málaga wine or Moscatel sherry
> 1 dessertspoon icing sugar
>
> **MANTECADOS** (makes about 20)
> 140g plain flour
> 40g whole blanched almonds
> 90g unsalted butter
> 60g caster sugar
> 1 teaspoon ground cinnamon

Mix the strawberries with the Moscatel and icing sugar to taste, and marinate in the fridge for a few hours.

Preheat the oven to 190°C/375°F/Gas 5.

Brown the flour in a tray on the top shelf of the preheated oven for about 20 minutes until beige in colour. Roast the almonds until light brown, then grind as fine as possible. Beat the butter and sugar together until soft, pale and fluffy, then add the almonds, cinnamon and flour. Pack the mixture together on a flat surface so it is about 1.5cm thick, and with a sherry glass or round pastry cutter about 3cm in diameter cut out little rounds. Place these on a baking tray lined with greaseproof paper, and bake for 30–45 minutes on the middle shelf of the preheated oven until golden. Remove and cool completely.

Serve the strawberries in a bowl with the Moscatel syrup and the mantecados on the side.

Helado de pasas de Málaga
MALAGA RAISIN ICE-CREAM

Although a very simple recipe using a basic custard for the ice-cream, all the complexity and flavour comes from the sherry. For the raisins are soaked in Pedro Ximénez sherry, the treacly, sweet, raisiny sherry made from Pedro Ximénez grapes, that are first dried in the sun to concentrate their sugar and flavour.

Serves 8 (makes just over 1 litre)
> 600ml double cream
> 300ml milk
> 1 small cinnamon stick
> 1 vanilla pod
> 7 egg yolks
> 85g caster sugar
> 100g raisins covered with 100ml Pedro Ximénez sherry
> or Pedro Ximénez Malaga wine (see Sherry Suppliers)

Place the cream, milk and cinnamon stick in a large saucepan. Split the vanilla pod in half lengthways and scrape the tiny seeds into the pan. Heat until just below boiling point, then remove from the stove. Beat the egg yolks and sugar together for 5–10 minutes until pale and thick. Loosen the egg with a little of the cream/milk mixture, then pour the egg back into the saucepan, scraping the bowl out with a spatula. Whisk well to mix everything properly and return to a low heat, stirring constantly. Heat gently to cook out the egg but be careful not to curdle it. When the mixture thickens and just before it bubbles, remove from the heat, pour into a bowl and place over iced water to cool.

Churn in an ice-cream machine (in batches if necessary), adding the raisins and sherry towards the end of the churning. For those without an ice-cream machine, try freezing the ice-cream by hand, but remember to stir every half-hour to prevent crystallisation. Stirring will also help distribute the raisins evenly as they tend to sink to the bottom before the custard hardens enough to suspend them. This process will take about 2 hours, depending on the temperature of your freezer.

Serve with a chilled glass of Pedro Ximénez on the side or poured over the ice-cream.

Chocolate and apricot tart

For this tart we use amber sheets of apricot paste called 'amradeen' or 'apricot leather'. This Lebanese and Syrian speciality is traditionally used in ice-creams or as an Arab sweet for children. It has a slightly tart finish (although this can vary), which is important so it cuts through the rich chocolate. If you cannot find apricot paste, use dried apricots instead.

Serves 6

> 1 x Sweet Pastry Tart Shell (see page 262)
>
> **FILLING**
> 180g apricot paste (see **Lebanese and Turkish Suppliers**) or dried
>   apricots
> 4 tablespoons water
> 2 tablespoons lemon juice
> 135g unsalted butter
> 110g dark chocolate (like Valrhona, 70% cocoa solids), broken up
> 2 large eggs
> 60g caster sugar

Follow the instructions on page 262 for cooking the pastry shell, then remove to a rack and cool. Preheat the oven to 180°C/350°F/Gas 4.

To start the filling, place the apricot paste in a saucepan over a low heat with the water and lemon juice, and stir until a smooth paste is formed. If using dried apricots, chop them very finely, then transfer to a saucepan and simmer for about 5 minutes with the same amount of water and lemon (if required) until soft. Purée in a blender. The mixture should taste slightly tart. Spread the apricot on the base of the tart shell, and leave to cool for a short while until the apricot forms a slight skin.

Meanwhile, place the butter and chocolate in a bain-marie and heat. When the chocolate has melted, whisk the eggs and sugar together until pale, light and fluffy. Fold the eggs and chocolate/butter together, pour into the tart shell and even out with a spatula. Bake on the middle shelf of the pre-heated oven for about 25 minutes. The filling should still be a little wobbly when you take it out, and have a very thin crust on top. Serve with creamy yoghurt or crème fraîche.

Rosewater and orange-blossom water

Rosewater and orange-blossom water are two of the better-known ingredients of the Middle East. Both are made from distilled petals, rosewater from a particular type of rose called ward al-joori in Arabic, and orange-blossom water from the flowers of the bitter Seville orange. They are used in a number of puddings, syrups and rice dishes. Available in most Middle Eastern shops.

Rosewater and cardamom ice-cream

This ice-cream is not to everyone's liking, but those who appreciate the exotic, heavenly scent of rosewater will adore it. The secret is to make a sugar syrup to sweeten the cream, but instead of using water, we substitute rosewater. The addition of gum mastic, a resin from a tree native to Greece and Turkey, makes this ice-cream even more exotic.

Serves 8

 2 tablespoons whole green cardamoms

 600ml milk

 600ml double cream

 1 cinnamon stick

 160g caster sugar

 230ml rosewater

 3 crystals gum mastic, crushed with 1 teaspoon caster sugar
  (optional, see Turkish and Greek Suppliers)

 1 x 400ml tin evaporated milk

 dried rose petals (optional, see Iranian Suppliers)

Lightly crush the cardamom pods in a mortar and pestle, and pick out as much of the green pod as you can, leaving behind the small black seeds. Pound the seeds to a fine powder.

Pour the milk and cream into a large saucepan, and add the ground cardamom and the cinnamon stick. Bring to the boil and then simmer over a medium heat, stirring occasionally, until the liquid has reduced by about a quarter and has turned a rich creamy colour similar to evaporated milk (around 20 minutes).

Meanwhile in a small saucepan dissolve the sugar in the rosewater over a low heat and simmer until a thin syrup is formed. Remove from the heat and allow to cool.

When the milk and cream are ready, remove from the heat, strain out the cinnamon and discard. Stir in the crushed gum mastic (if using), and cool for 10–15 minutes. Add the evaporated milk and combine with the rosewater syrup. Churn in an ice-cream machine (or freeze by hand, see page 271). We serve this ice-cream with a few dried rose petals on top; buy these from Iranian shops, but they are more for aesthetics than flavour.

Yoghurt cake with pistachios

This Lebanese pudding is delicious warm or chilled. Some fruit on the side, although not necessary, is a nice addition - cherries in June to July, or pomegranate seeds in December. If you do not make your own yoghurt, use a mixture of Greek strained yoghurt and normal yoghurt, or Greek yoghurt thinned with a little milk.

Serves 6

>   3 large organic or free-range eggs, separated
>   70g caster sugar
>   2 vanilla pods, split in half lengthways
>   350g yoghurt
>   finely grated zest of 1 lemon and ½ orange
>   juice of 1 lemon
>   20g plain flour
>   30g shelled unsalted pistachio nuts, roughly chopped

Preheat the oven to 180°C/350°F/Gas 4, and put a bain-marie of water in to warm on the middle shelf. Have ready a 25cm round or square baking dish or cake tin with a solid bottom, preferably stainless-steel, or lined with greaseproof paper.

In a bowl beat the egg yolks with three-quarters of the sugar until thick and pale. Scrape out the seeds from the vanilla pod and mix into the egg-sugar mixture. Add the yoghurt, lemon and orange zest, lemon juice and the flour and mix well. In a separate bowl whisk up the egg whites with the remaining sugar until soft peaks form. Gently and evenly, fold the whites into the yoghurt mixture. Pour the mixture into the baking tin. Place the tin in the bain-marie, making sure that the boiling water comes halfway up the tin, and cook for about 20 minutes. Then add the chopped pistachios, sprinkling them gently on top, and continue cooking for a further 20 minutes or until the top is light brown in colour. The correct consistency of the cake should be a light sponge on top with a wet custard below. Serve with yoghurt.

Bitter chocolate, coffee and cardamom truffle cake

The flavours of chocolate, coffee and cardamom work very well in this rich and luxurious cake. It is easy to make but one must never be tempted to over-whip the cream as it will ruin the texture.

Serves 8-10
>   340g dark chocolate (like Valrhona, 70% cocoa solids), broken up
>   400ml milk
>   30g green cardamom pods, crushed
>   2 level tablespoons instant coffee
>   2 tablespoons caster sugar
>   800ml double cream
>   65g roasted almonds, roughly chopped

Have ready a 20cm cake tin lined with clingfilm or greaseproof paper.

Place the chocolate in a bowl to melt in a bain-marie. Meanwhile, reduce the milk with the cardamom by a third until dark creamy yellow. Strain. Add the coffee to the hot milk and some sugar to balance out the bitterness. (The amount of sugar needed may vary due to the bitterness of the coffee or chocolate.) Whip the cream until it just begins to thicken. It is very important to stop whipping the second the cream begins to thicken otherwise you may ruin the final texture of the cake. You will also notice the cream thickens when warm chocolate is added. Gently fold the melted chocolate and milk/coffee mixtures into it. (Do not mix the chocolate and coffee mixture beforehand, as the coffee tends to crystallise the chocolate.)

Cover the base of the tin with the almonds, spoon the chocolate mixture on top and chill for about an hour until firm and set. Alternatively you can sprinkle the almonds over the cake once you have taken it out of its mould. Serve with yoghurt or crème fraîche.

Walnut, lemon and cardamom cake

This moist, crumbly cake is also delicious as a tea cake.

Serves 6

> 230g butter
> 230g caster sugar
> 175g walnuts, chopped, some very fine, some rough
> 175g whole blanched almonds, some very fine, some rough
> 3 eggs
> 160g polenta
> 1 level teaspoon baking powder
> finely grated zest of 1½ lemons
> juice of 2 large lemons
> 3–4 level teaspoons ground cardamom seeds

Preheat the oven to 160°C/325°F/Gas 3. Have ready a 25cm spring-form tin lined with greaseproof paper, and place this on a baking sheet.

Beat the butter and sugar together until light and very pale. Stir in the walnuts and almonds, then the eggs, one at a time. Add the polenta, baking powder, lemon zest and juice, and cardamom to taste. There should be a nice balance between the lemon and cardamom. Spoon the mixture into the prepared tin, place the baking sheet in the preheated oven, and bake for about 1½ hours until the cake is golden brown on top and just firm in the middle. Remove from the oven and cool on a rack before opening the tin.

Suppliers

The following addresses should enable you to find specialist ingredients. Some delis may order you things in even if they don't have them in stock, so don't be afraid to ask! Wholefood shops are often good for dried pulses and nuts.

LONDON

SPANISH

Alsur
Tel: 020 7686 4885
Contact: Hannah

Brindisa
Wholesale and general enquiries
Tel: 020 8772 1600
Brindisa at Borough Market
(Fridays & Saturdays, 9am–5pm)
London Bridge
London SE1 9EL
Tel: 020 7403 6932
Retail website:
www.tapas.co.uk
Brindisa at 32 Exmouth Market, London EC1R 4QE

R. Garcia and Sons
248 Portobello Road
London W11 1LL
Tel: 020 7221 6119

Javier de la Serna
Tel: 020 7272 9876
Fax: 020 7263 6283
email: javier@delaserna.freeserve.co.uk

La Coruna
103 Newington Butts
London SE1 6SF
Tel: 020 7703 3165

Rias Altas
97 Frampton Street
London NW8 8NA
Tel: 020 7262 4340

Stefano Vallebona
Tel: 020 8877 0903
www.lascorpacciata.com
(Cured fish roe, bottarga)

PORTUGUESE

Lisboa Delicatessen
54 Golborne Road
London W10 5NR
Tel: 020 8969 1052
(good for salt cod)

MIDDLE EASTERN

Arch Impex
Tel: 020 8961 5116
Contact: Haddad
(wholesale)

La Belle Boucherie
3–5 Bell Street
London NW1 5BY
Tel: 020 7258 0230

Damas Gate
81–85 Uxbridge Road
London W12 5BY
Tel: 020 8743 5116

LEBANESE

Archie
14 Moscow Road
London W2 4AH
Tel: 020 7229 2275

Green Valley
36 Upper Berkeley St
London W1H 7PG
Tel: 020 7402 7385

Lebanese Food Centre
153 The Vale, Acton,
London W3 7RH
Tel: 020 8740 7365

Zen
27 Moscow Road
London W2 4AH
Tel: 020 7792 2058

MOROCCAN

Le Maroc
94 Golborne Road
London W10 5PS
Tel: 020 8968 9783

Le Marrakech
64 Golborne Road
London W10 5PS
Tel: 020 8964 8307

TURKISH

TFC Dalston Ltd
89 Ridley Road
London E8 2NP
Tel: 020 7254 6754

TFC Leytonstone Ltd
647–661 High Road

London E11 4RD
Tel: 020 8558 8149

TFC Haringey Ltd
385–387 Green Lanes
London N4 1EU
Tel: 020 8340 4547

TFC Lewisham Ltd
227–229 Lewisham High Street, London SE13
Tel: 020 8318 0436

TFC Croydon Ltd
73–77 London Road
West Croydon CR0 2RF
Tel: 020 8681 7631

Yasar Halim
493–495 Green Lanes
London N4 1A1
Tel: 020 8340 8090

Yasar Halim
182 Uxbridge Road
London W12 7GP
Tel: 020 8740 9477

CYPRIOT/GREEK

T. Adamou & Sons
124–126 Chiswick High Road, London W4 1PU
Tel: 020 8994 0752

Andreas Michli & Son
33 Salusbury Road
London N4 1JY
Tel: 020 8802 0188

IRANIAN/PERSIAN

Khayam Supermarket
149 Seymour Place
London W1H 5TL
Tel: 020 7258 3637

Reza Pâtisserie
345 Kensington High Street, London W8 6NW
Tel: 020 7602 3674
Mail order tel: 020 7603 0924

Sorour
101 Robin Hood Way
Kingston Vale

Super Bahar
394a Kensington High Street, London W8 6NW
Tel: 020 7603 5083

GENERAL SELECTION

Bluebird Food Market
350 Kings Road
London SW3 5UU
Tel: 020 7559 1153

Harvey Nichols
Fifth Floor Food Market
London SW1X 7RJ
Tel: 020 7235 5000

Maquis Delicatessen
111 Hammersmith Grove,
London W6
(Good selection of Spanish and Muslim Mediterranean ingredients)

Mortimer & Bennett
33 Turnham Green Terrace, Chiswick,
London W4 1RG
Tel: 020 8995 4145

Selfridges Food Hall
400 Oxford Street
London W1A 1AB
Tel: 020 7629 1234

OUTSIDE LONDON

BRISTOL

Chandos Deli
6 Princess Victoria Street,
Clifton, Bristol BS8 4BP
Tel: 0117 974 3275
www.chandos.deli.com
(General selection, especially Spanish)

CAMBRIDGE

Cambridge Cheese Co.
All Saints Passage
Cambridge CB2 3LS
Tel: 01223 328 672
(General selection)

EDINBURGH
Valvona & Crolla
19 Elm Row
Edinburgh EH7 4AA
Tel: 0131 556 6066
www.valvonacrolla.
co.uk (General selection;
mail order)

GLASGOW
Andreas Greek
Delicatessen
27 Old Dumbarton Road
Glasgow G3 8RD
Tel: 0141 576 5031
www.andreasgreekdeli.
freeserve.co.uk
(Greek/Cypriot)

I.J. Mellis
492 Great Western Road
Kelvinbridge, Glasgow
G12 8EW
Tel: 0141 339 8998
(Fabulous cheese, also a
few Spanish ingredients)

Scherezade
47 Bank Street, Hillhead,
Glasgow G12 8NE
Tel: 0141 334 2121
(Middle Eastern)

HEREFORDSHIRE
Hay Wholefoods & Deli
Lion Street, Hay-on-Wye,
Herefordshire HR3 5AA
Tel: 01497 820 708
(General selection)

KENT
Williams and Brown
Delicatessen
28a Harbour Street
Whitstable CT5 1AH
Tel: 01227 274 507
(Mainly Spanish)

LEEDS
Harvey Nichols Food
Market
107-111 Briggate
Leeds LS1 6AZ
Tel: 0113 204 8888
(General selection)

LINCOLNSHIRE
Simpole Clarke
10 St Paul's Street
Stamford, Lincolnshire

PE9 2BE
Tel: 01780 480 646
www.simpole-clarke.com
(Good general selection,
also mail order)

LIVERPOOL
No. 7 Delicatessen
15 Faulkner Street
Liverpool
Tel: 0151 709 9633
(A few Spanish things)

MANCHESTER
Selfridges Food Hall
1 The Dome
The Trafford Centre
Manchester M17 8DA
Tel: 0161 629 1234
(General selection)

Atlas Delicatessen
345 Deansgate
Manchester M3 4LG
Tel: 0161 834 2266
(General selection)

NORTH YORKSHIRE
Arcimboldos
146 Kings Road
Harrogate HG1 5HY
Tel: 01423 508 760
(General selection)

SHREWSBURY
Appleyards Delicatessen
85 Wyle Cop
Shrewsbury S1 1UT
Tel: 01743 240 180
(General selection)

SOMERSET
Olive Garden Delicatessen
91 Hill Road, Clevedon,
North Somerset
BS21 7PN
Tel: 01275 341 222
(Especially Spanish)

SUPERMARKETS
Sainsbury's (Special
Selection): smoked
paprika, judión beans,
Cabernet Sauvignon
vinegar, sherry vinegar,
paella rice, saffron, dried
mushrooms, membrillo,
pomegranate molasses
and more
Waitrose: warka (brik)
pastry

FARMERS' MARKETS
For a full list nationwide,
send a SAE to:
National Association of
Farmers' Markets
South Vault, Green Park
Station, Green Park,
Bath BA1 1JB

OLIVES (and preserved
lemons)
The Fresh Olive Oil
Company of Provence Ltd.
Mail Order. Tel: 020 8453
1918

MORTARS AND
PESTLES
John Julian Design
Tel: 020 7249 6969
www.johnjuliandesign.com

Sherry

Below are a few notes on
the classic sherry styles
(see also page 34) and our
favourite examples.

FINO
Ranging from green tast-
ing and wine-like to the
stronger and older styles.
Fino is always fresh, dry
and drunk very cold,
either as an aperitif or
with a starter.

TIO PEPE (Gonzalez
Byass): Hard to fault,
easy to drink. Start here
to decide if you enjoy fino.
Despite the volume of
production, Tio Pepe is
still a wine made with
integrity. Widely available

INOCENTE (Valdespino):
An old friend and Moro's
house fino. A big old style
with much class.
Oddbins Fine Wine
Lea & Sandeman Ltd

LA INA (Allied Domecq):
A well-made, enjoyable
wine of medium age and
strength.
Unwins off-licence: head
office tel: 01322 272 711
R. Garcia & Sons Ltd

DON ZOILO This deli-
cious fino of medium age
has a particularly good
bouquet of a bodega.
F. & E. May Ltd (Wines
Direct)

MANZANILLA Same
wine as fino but it resides
by the sea. The humid
salty air subtly affects the
wine, giving it a salty
tang. To be drunk very
cold as an aperitif or with
a starter.

MANZANILLA
DELICIOSA (Valdespino):
Beautifully made wine
with a stronger older
style which is complex
and tangy. (Moro's house
manzanilla)
Oddbins Fine Wine
Lea & Sandeman Ltd

LA GITANA (Hidalgo):
Well-rounded and
flavoursome.
Oddbins (nationwide)
Waitrose supermarkets
R. Garcia & Sons Ltd

LA GOYA (Delgado
Zuleta): Deliciously tangy,
classy wine.
Dukes of Ingleton
J.W. Martinez-Perez Ltd
R.S. Wines Ltd
The Bristol Wine
Merchant
R. Garcia & Sons Ltd
Peter Watts Wines
Springfield Wines
Vins de Bordeaux (Winos)
Vino Vita

LA GUITA (Rainera
Perez Maria): Lighter
style but by no means
thin. Refreshing and
delicious.
Budgens Store: tel: 0208
422 9511

SOLEAR (BARBADILLO)
A fresh, slightly green
taste with a salty tang.
Fenwicks tel: 0207 629
9161

Selfridges tel: 0207 629 1234
Victoria Wine tel: 01483 71 50 66
Wine Rack tel: 0207 253 2908
Unwins tel: 01322 272 711
Threshers tel: 01707 328 244

PASADA PASTRANA

(HIDALGO) A strong wilful wine with amazing length and character. When in Jerez we were told that this slightly oxidised older style of manzanilla was once common; now it is something of a rarity.
Oddbins Fine Wine

HEREDEROS DE ARGUESO: This is

another Pasada style manzanilla which we are very fond of. Again amazing freshness, character and length. Difficult to get hold of.

AMONTILLADO

With amontillado, the mother fungus (flor) on the fino is allowed to die. No longer protected, the wine is allowed to oxidise, hence its amber colour. Amontillado is traditionally a dry wine with a hint of caramel and nuttiness. All of these amontillados are rarer, older styles and therefore not the cheapest, but we maintain still good value. Cheaper amontillados to our taste can be thin and acidic. To be drunk chilled or at room temperature.

TIO DIEGO (Valdespino) Very dry with a bold flavour and good length.
Lea & Sandeman Ltd

AMONTILLADO DEL DUQUE (Gonzalez Byass): Smooth and classy with some

sweetness but with a clean dry finish.
Oddbins Fine Wine

ROYAL AMBRASANTE
Dry Amontillado (Sandeman): A delicious well-made wine with a slight sweetness but a clean finish.
Oddbins Fine Wine

OLOROSO

Ranging from dry, complex and strong to velvety and fruity with some sweetness, but should always have a clean and uncloying finish. A richer slightly old style which sometimes has the sweeter Pedro Ximénez grape added to it. To be drunk chilled or at room temperature.

DRY OLOROSO (Don Zoilo): Nutty, dry, clean and light.
F. & E. May Ltd (Wines Direct)

DON GONZALO (Valdespino): Dry, complex and strong. An evocative, grown-up sherry.
Lea & Sandeman Ltd

SOLERA 1842 (Valdespino): Treads a most brilliant line between being sweet and dry. Smooth, complex and delicious taste.
Oddbins Fine Wine
Lea & Sandeman Ltd

ROYAL CORREGIDOR (Sandeman): Rich, well-balanced, delicious wine.
Oddbins Fine Wine

MATUSALEM APOSTOLES (Gonzalez Byass): Smooth with a wonderful taste of dried fruit.
Oddbins Fine Wine

PALO CORTADO A

dry wine ranging from austere and complex to soft and rounded with some fruit. Starts life as an amontillado but takes on the palate and colour of an oloroso. A very small percentage of sherries transfer themselves into palo cortado. To be drunk chilled or at room temperature.

PALO CORTADO DEL CARRASCAL (Valdespino): Incredible nose with a bouquet of the bodega. Intensely strong, not easy to drink, but fascinating.
Oddbins Fine Wine
Lea & Sandeman Ltd

PALO CORTADO, RARE, SOLERA (Sandeman): Rich, velvety, delicious wine with medium sweetness. A wonderful wine.

PEDRO XIMÉNEZ

The definitive raisiny grape and wine. It is always sweet, but good wines have complexity. To be drunk chilled or at room temperature.

PEDRO XIMÉNEZ SUPERIOR (Valdespino): Wonderfully raisiny. The wine we use for our Malaga raisin ice-cream.
Oddbins Fine Wine
Lea & Sandeman Ltd

NOË PEDRO XIMÉNEZ (Gonzalez Byass): Raisiny with some flavour of liquorice and burnt caramel.
Oddbins Fine Wine

ROYAL ESMERALDA
Classic, perfect PX.
Oddbins Fine Wine

SHERRY SUPPLIERS

For any further enquiries concerning sherry, contact The Sherry Institute on 020 7486 0101.

ODDBINS FINE WINE STORES

Wines can be bought over the phone at these branches and collected from your local Oddbins.

London:
57 Lombard Rd
London SW11 3RX
Tel: 020 7738 1013
Fax: 020 7738 1247

41a Farringdon St
London EC4A 4AN
Tel: 020 7329 6989
Fax: 020 7248 9916

141 Notting Hill Gate
London W11 3LB
Tel: 020 7243 8668
Fax: 020 7229 2978

Cambridge
14 Regent St
Cambridge CB2 1DB
Tel: 01223 358843
Fax: 01223 460836

Edinburgh
5 Queensferry St
Edinburgh EH2 4PD
Tel: 0131 225 5707
Fax: 0131 225 9656

Glasgow
93 Mitchell St
Glasgow G11 7RT
Tel: 0141 221 3294
Fax: 0141 221 4776

Oxford
7 Little Clarendon St
Oxford OX1 2HP
Tel: 01865 310 807
Fax: 01865 510 023

LONDON
F. & E. May Ltd (Wines Direct)
Viaduct House
16 Warner St
(18 Rosebery Avenue)

London EC1R 5HA
Tel: 020 7843 1600
Fax: 020 7843 1601

R. Garcia & Sons Ltd
248 Portobello Rd
London W11 1LL
Tel: 020 7221 6119

Lea & Sandeman Ltd
170 Fulham Rd
London SW10 9PR
Tel: 020 7244 0522
Fax: 020 7244 0533

211 Kensington Church St
London W8 7LX
Tel: 020 7221 1982
Fax: 020 7221 1985

51 Barnes High St
London SW13 9LN

Tel: 020 8878 8643
Fax: 020 8878 6522
email:Sales@leaand-sandeman.co.uk

BRISTOL
Bristol Wine Merchant
Arch no.9 Berkeley Court
Earl Russell Way,
Lawrence Hill
Bristol BS5 0RX
Tel: 0117 935 0143

R.S. Wines Ltd
Avonleigh
Parklands Road
Bower Ashton
Bristol BS3 2JW
Tel: 0117 963 1780

CHELTENHAM
Seasonal Specifics

22 Andover Rd
Cheltenham
Gloucestershire
Tel: 01242 529 862

ESSEX
Peter Watts Wines
Wisdom's Barn, Colne Rd
Coggeshall
Essex CO6 1TD
Tel: 01376 561 130

KENT
Vino Vita
61 High St, Sidcup
Kent DH14 6ED
Tel: 020 8302 7151

LANCASHIRE
Vins de Bordeaux (Winos)
63 George St, Oldham
Greater Manchester

Lancashire OL1 1LX
Tel: 0161 652 9396

NORTH YORKSHIRE
Dukes of Ingleton
6 High St, Ingleton
North Yorkshire LA6 3EB
Tel: 01524 241 738

WEST YORKSHIRE
J.W. Martinez-Perez Ltd
35 The Grove, Ilkley
West Yorkshire LS29 9NJ
Tel: 01943 816 515

Springfield Wines
Springfield Mill
Norman Rd, Denby Dale
Huddersfield
West Yorkshire HD8 8TH
Tel: 01484 864 929

Vegetables and fruit in season

(underscored – Mediterranean, normal – British)

ARTICHOKES, GLOBE: November–April

ARTICHOKES, JERUSALEM: October–December

ASPARAGUS: March–April, May–mid June

AUBERGINES: May–September

BEANS, BROAD: mid March/April–May, June–July

BEANS, GREEN: August–September

BEANS, RUNNER: August–September

BEETROOT (small with leaves): May–August

BLACKBERRIES: August–September

CARROTS: April/May–July/August

CHARD: summer and spring

COURGETTES: May–July, August–September

FENNEL: November–January

GARLIC LEAVES, wild: March–April

GRAPES: September–November

LEMONS: December–February

MANGOES: Alfonso from Pakistan, May–June

MUSHROOMS, WILD: September–November

ORANGES, Seville and blood: December–February

PEAS: mid March–April

PEPPERS: July/August

POMEGRANATES: October–January

POTATOES, NEW: June–August

PUMPKIN/SQUASH: September–November

QUINCES: September–November, October, November

RADISHES: summer

RASPBERRIES: August–September

SPRING GREENS: February–April

SPROUTING BROCCOLI: February–April

STRAWBERRIES: August–September

SWEETCORN: June–July, August–September

TOMATOES: April–July, July–September

TURNIPS (small with leaves): April–June

Index

Kevin Francis Gray

For Luke

The authors would like to thank: our partner Mark Sainsbury, Jake Hodges, Caz Hildebrand, Denise Bates, Susan Fleming, Pia Tryde, Pat Kavanagh, Ciara Lunn, Sarah Barlow and Daemienne Sheehan for additional editorial help, Toby Glanville and Kevin Francis Gray for help with photography, Rose Gray, Lidia Flores, Julian Sainsbury, Danny McSorley, Tony Calderbank, Sarah Clarke, Colette Clark, Laura Jeffreys, Wilde Fry, Rose and Dominic Prince, Alex and Katie Clarke, Linn Lee, Tony and Sabrina Fry, Teddy Clarke, Charlie and Sonamara Jeffreys, Christopher and Anna Jeffreys, Engin Akýn, Sam and Jeannie Chesterton, and all our chefs, especially Oliver Rowe, Jacob Kenedy, Sylvain Jamois, Kevin Francis Gray, Lisa Armour Brown, and the whole team past and present at Moro.

The publishers would like to thank the following for permission to reproduce photographs in this book: Bridgeman Art Library/Bibliothèque Nationale, Paris: endpapers; Hulton Getty: 21, 35 (top and bottom right), 135, 201, 227; Toby Glanville: author photograph on jacket; Kevin Francis Gray: 288; Oronoz: 107; Popperfoto: 9, 35 (left), 77, 177, 261. All other photographs are by Pia Tryde.

Moro restaurant is at 34–36 Exmouth Market, London EC1 Tel: 020 7833 8336.